HEALTH AND CULTURE OF A METROPOLITAN RESETTLEMENT

HEALTH AND CULTURE OF A METROPOLITAN RESETTLEMENT

ISSUES AND CHALLENGES

K.K. Ganguly

RAJAT PUBLICATIONS

New Delhi

Health and Culture of a Metropolitan Resettlement: Issues and Challenges
by *K.K. Ganguly*

This edition is published by Rajat Publications
4740/23, Ansari Road Daryaganj,
New Delhi - 110002

ISBN: 978-81-7880-036-3

Edition 2026

Printed and bound in India

RAJAT
PUBLICATIONS

4740/23, Ansari Road, Daryaganj,
New Delhi- 110002 (India)
Mob:- +91-9811484973, +91-9811105389
E-mail: rajat_publication@yahoo.com

This Book is Dedicated to

My Parents

My Siblings

My Wife and Daughter

PREFACE

Since independence, the social scientists in India have taken lot of interest in working in different national health programmes and given sociological inputs in few of those programmes as well. They have tried to understand the link between health services and the community. But very often they could not tackle the issue successfully.

It has been lately realised that concepts and methods required to study the complex issues in the field of community health by the social scientists are to be integrated thread bare with the society and its various norms and culture. And, it has to be interdisciplinary in nature. For instance even to study patients in a hospital who is only one of the components of a highly complex social and technological system, social scientists need to study, such, diverse areas as cultural adjustment and coping mechanism of different groups of patients within the hospital, their illness behaviour, sick role performance and perceptions, attitude of patients towards different services that are offered to them. Similarly, research on community's involvement in health care service, health institution and health practices, besides understanding the total life style of the community. Health services, promotive, preventive, curative and rehabilitative are key factors for improving the health status of any society. Economic status, nutrition, water supply and other environmental conditions, educations, and social as well as political relations are some of the other factors which influence the health status of a community equally if not less. The intrinsic dynamics of a society, which are so important in determining the status of the health and health services, have their roots in the cultural, ecological and historical background of the society.

Human groups interact with their surroundings to develop their own ways of life-their culture includes mode of production and social relations. The consideration of social ecological setting is also important in analysing the generation of health problems within a human group, social ecological conditions also mediate between the disease causative agents and the individuals and are often direct causative agents. Obviously, because of specific ecological and historical considerations, different modes of production and production relations, the human groups differ in their socio-cultural status of a community defines the limits of its health and health services development along with its health culture.

The life of the slum community resettled in Jahangirpuri, Delhi, stimulated the scholar to undertake the study and to find out how far the professional, elite oriented, bureaucratic and technocratic health care delivery system of the metropolis have been able to deliver the goods. Besides, its impact on the health culture of the people.

The people of the resettlement and the village deserve the share of their health care needs fulfilled. But it was appalling to note that the resettlers were utterly neglected in terms of their fulfilment of unmet felt need, in terms of getting a decent life outside their respective hometowns. Moreover, gradual decadence of their plight was very clear and obvious through the study. These people inherited certain skills to live an independent successful life, but its was sheer tryst with their destiny that not only they lost every skill to live healthy and die peacefully but they also lost the hope of learning or regaining anything good or meaningful for their own life as well as for their progeny.

An alternative has been suggested due course of the study in this work. However, one need to test the validity of the same so far.

I acknowledge the Rajat Publications for their effort to bring out this book.

K.K. Ganguly

CONTENTS

1

INTRODUCTION

Evolution of Health Services in India

Health and human development form an integral component of overall socio-economic development of any nation. According to World Health Organisation (WHO), "health, which is state of complete physical mental, social and religious well being", not merely the absence of illness or disease. The first committee which came to existence on the eve of independence (1946) was known as *Bhore Committee* or "Health Survey and Development Committee, tried to keep up with the guidelines of the WHO, to improve the Indian health scenario.[1] The prime task of the committee was to give the health status of Indians a scientific and systematic fillip by implementing a series of well integrated policies, i.e. access to health care for all, more close and people oriented services, people's motivation and orientation for better and concerted preventive health care practice. More and more knowledge of preventive and social medicine is highly essential and desirable to make doctors more people oriented was also stressed by the recommendation of the committee. It is note worthy that, various short and long term programmes meant for primary health centres and sub-centre in rural areas as well as number of beds and doctors proposed to cater the people were proportionate to the population of the country. In other words, the logistics and health man power lay out was given a formal shape for the first time.

Subsequently, in 1961, the first health and manpower review committee of independent India came into existance under Dr. Mudaliar.[2] It emphasised to invigorate and implement the commitments of the former committee. Thereafter, the Kartar Singh Committee[3] of 1973 laid emphasis on retention of unipurpose workers as multipurpose workers in order to carry out the various national health programmes.

Shrivastava Committee[4] of 1975 followed the Kartar Singh Committee, and stressed for giving boost to appropriate medical education as per the requirement of the country and right kind of supportive health man power to be evolved which could take care of the recommendation of previous committees. In 1981, a joint committee report of ICMR[5] and ICSSR was presented on revamped health care and health manpower status in concordance with the "Alma Ata" declaration of 1978. As late as 1983, "National Health Policy was evolved which tried to encompass all the previous committees recommedation besides a few new ideas needed to make a better and comprehensive health policy."[6] The policy stated the need for well dispersed net work of primary health care services along with more organised manpower, more dissemination of simple technology to health volunteers, self reliance and effective community participation, good referral system, more planned technology and manpower in health for better services, more allocation of funds for voluntary agencies. More equipped Primary and Sub-centres for treatment, fixation of priorities for treatment for difficult areas i.e. hilly or tribal area. And finally, it recommended for "health team approach".

The reports of the committees were intended to assess, appraise and to evolve or modify appropriate health programme for the country as per the requirement of the people from time to time.

But, on the whole the reports considered health and health care as the advancement of health care logistics in order to give a technologically sound health care treatment, viz. the advance CCT and X-ray machines and other hardwares, buildings, equipment supplies, vehicles and so on. Bedrock of such developments have built in philosophy of institutional health care model to serve the patients more technically rather than humanely. Hence, healthy living is possible only when there is no disease and the cure of the disease can be had only in institutions of health care delivery replete with such infrastructure. It was felt by the planners of health policy that there should be institutes of supper specialisation in every big cities to detect and deal with pathogens of ailment through a series of highly technologically evolved machines. Thus came the institutes of super specialisation.

This could be understood more clearly in the words of Bernard and Illich[7] as they put it, "the clinical paradigm has defined disease and health for centuries. This paradigm take individual physiology as the norm for pathology (as contrasted with broader social conditions) and locates sickness in the individuals body, a typical nineteenth century variant held that every illness was disturbance, exaggeration, diminution or cessation of a corresponding normal function" (Bernard, 1965). This paradigm of treatment readjusted the body until its physiological norm was restored, a mechanistic approach that reduced the body to a machine whose organs could be discretely examined and regulated, implicit in this notion was the concept of health care advancement. Illich[8] has further emphasised that, "the medical quantifiers of the nineteenth century placed sickness in the centre of medical system that was a mechanical frame work for the investigation of the mechanical troubles of the human body (Illich 1975). As Illich has rightly pointed out... "the proximate source of the clinical paradigm was the hospital base of the medical perception of reality. During the nineteenth century, the hospital became the place where diseased people were housed, diseases were identified and census of diseases were kept. Along with sickness, health acquired a clinical status becoming the absence of clinical symptoms. Initially, the clinical paradigm appeared in association with disease, but eventually, came to dominate the entire spectrum. One way to approach the spread of the clinical medical paradigm — a phenomenon sometime referred to as the medicalisation of society — is to arrange various medical disciplines on a continuum extending from death at one end to health at the other."

Of late, after the Alma Ata declaration a people oriented health policy was envisaged in ICMR and ICSSR joint committee report in 1981 (Although, on paper a community oriented health care approach was talked of in Bhore Committee report of 1946). Since, independence upto 1980 a clear rise in hospitals, doctors, specialists can be observed. An upsurge in medical manpower and logistics was defined by expert like Jeffery[9] as,.... "Efforts continue to be made in India to set the standards of medical education and research with reference to those prevailing in the west particularly the United Kingdom and the United States of America. Apart from the Medical Council of India other institutions have come up since independence which have consistently performed the role of champions of scientific progress that is western medicine in India."

Roger Jeffery puts the relationship of the Indian medical system and the British connection in the following words, "the relationship of dependency between doctors in India and the medical "establishment" in the West remained as such even after the derecognition of Indian medical degree by Britain."

Jeffery has gone to the extent of stating, such dependency on the west in the following words, "the predilection for technical aid may have been as much that of national decision makers as of foreign aid agencies. In sum, while external health aid has supported national priorities, it has perhaps been inadequately tuned to the national context" (Chatterjee M. 1988).[10] Moreover, since the independence the influence of the west seem to be strongly affecting the policy planner of this country.

Genesis of hospitals in India

The historic evidence of various destitute homes and infirmaries are replete since the reign of emperor Ashok and in the regime of subsequent rulers and dynasties as well. In the Moghul period, both the Indian and the Arabic/Persian type of health care systems and hospital, existed side by side.

The genesis of modern Indian hospital can be traced back to the year of 1506, when in Cochin, Francisco de-Almedia[11] had built the first western type of hospital. It was followed by the Royal Hospital at Goa in 1510 meant for the Portuguese soldiers and other Europeans only. In 1842, the same was turned into a medical school of medicine and surgery.

The British-East India Company had built its first hospital in 1664 in Madras, in Bombay in 1676 and in Calcutta in 1707-1908 respectively. And in 1804, there came up the first Mofussil hospital in Dacca (erstwhile E. Pakistan). By 1840, there were more than a dozen of such hospitals which came up in India (Megaw 1938).[12] First Medical school known as "Native Medical Institution" was established in Calcutta where both the Ayurvedic and Western medicines were taught (a precursor of teaching hospital).

Since 1846 to 1900, the hospital in India had come up in a rapid pace.

By the turn of 20th century, a good number of western hospitals, "Anglo-Saxon in spirit" but Indian in structure came up in India which treated upon the native patients and taught native students with profound western overtones. And made a handful of native experts of health care delivery, who were absolutely hospital oriented rather than being community oriented. By 1902, there were four full-fledged medical colleges in Calcutta, Madras, Bombay and Lahore along with twenty two medical schools governed by General Medical Council of United Kingdom.

Table: 1.1
Growth of Hospitals in Pre-Independent India

	Name of the Institution	*Year inception*
1.	Hyderabad Medical School. Hyderabad	1846
2.	King Edward Medical School, Indore	1846
3.	Agra Medical School	1854
4.	Medical School of Amritsar	1864
5.	Campbell Medical School, Calcutta	1873
6.	Temple Medical School, Patna	1874
7.	Orissa Medical School, Cuttak.	1875
8.	B.J. Medical School, Patna	1878
9.	Ahmedabad Medical School, Ahmedabad	1879
10.	Calcutta Medical School, Calcutta	1886
11.	Christian Medical School, Ludhiana	1894
12.	College of Physicians and Surgeons Bengal	1895
13.	Haffkine Institute of India, Bombay	1899
14.	Berriwhite Medical School, Assam	1900

Lady Harding Medical College, the first women's medical college came up in Delhi in 1916. All these institution were brought under Medical Council of India, formulated in 1933.

Between, 1950 to 1981, the number of hospitals in India rose from 30 to 6670 respectively. And during the same period, 15968 dispensaries and 5568 primary health centres were built, out of 6670 hospitals 106 were teaching hospitals (*Pocket Book of Health Statistics*. Govt. of India 1983).[13] Numerical rise of hospitals, dispensaries and primary health centres did not improve the health care service of the common man, nor did it change the spirit of the functionaries. Contrary it became an unorganised complex of mammoth health care delivery system.

All India Institute of Medical Sciences (AIIMS), built in 1956 epitomising Western model of health care (emulating Johns Hopkins of U.S.) first of its kind in India. AIIMS opened the vista for super specialisation and in the subsequent years other specialist institutes came up in the same mould in various parts of the country i.e. P.G.I.M.E.R; Chandigarh, JIPMER; Pondichery. And two more, institutes came up in late twentieth century Sanjay Gandhi Institute for Post Graduate Medical Education and Research in Lucknow and Indira Gandhi Institute for Post Graduate Medical Education and Research in Patna to deliver the best of western health care model in the country.

In spite of logistic and manpower development of these institutes, health care delivery of common man did not improve commensurately.

With a shift in policies of World Health Organisation (W.H.O.), United Nations International Children's Emergency Fund, (UNICEF) and other UN organisations it was realised in seventies in most of the developing countries including India that there is a need to take stock of the existing health care structure viz., institutions and the delivery system of health care. In other words to detect that whether these institutions are community oriented or not, a group of social scientists studied some aspects of health care delivery system, i.e. doctor patient relationship in hospital, inter and intra staff relationship within the four walls of the hospital, health care delivery system in government hospital vis-a-vis private hospital. While, assessing the role of hospital in health care, it was seen as key determinant, an unavoidable element of good health care. The studies carried out were able to assess the status and the role of the hospital staffs per se. The studies also found out that the hospital is a place where the patient approaches with lot of skepticism and undergoes a score of test and treatment in the form of passive recipient in order to get back to apparent normalcy.

Various issues the care seekers faced, when they visited the hospital was also issue of concern for many scholars. Are the hospitals accessible for all, if not why, was also dealt with by some scholars. Before, the study could be carried out a detailed assessment of available data is warranted. Although, the studies referred earlier were designed to assess the function and utility of the hospital and health care institutes in a greater detail instead of assessing the role of these institutes for true patient care. The hospitals and other health care institutes have not been studied as a social institution catering to the health needs of the community.

Review of Hospital Studies

In this connection, it becomes essential to discuss some of the studies carried out by various experts, wherein, they have tried to understand hospital in various ways, i.e. hospital functioning, doctor patient relationship. Hospital vis-a-vis the professionals there and their role performance. To name a few relevant studies one can mention the following, Mathur,[14] in her study of "Human Organisation of Hospital" has analysed the hospital as an ultimate health care model to guide and govern the disease and health of the patients. Patient is not supposed to demand but to resign to his faith meekly while seeking health care. Many scholars studied and analysed the hospital health care in the light of "Parson and Fox Model"[15] (1952), has four components, two rights and two obligations, the rights to switch from ordinary life roles and to expect treatment, the obligation is to accept treatment and strive for recovery (has very little relevance in Indian situation, as it is an ethnocentric model). Similarly, Kirkpatrick[16] in her study of, "The delivery of health services in north India" has tried to find out the interaction of social structure at two levels viz, primary versus secondary, where primary is the people or patient who are inmate and secondary are the staff of the hospital, although, the study attempted to find out the gap between the two levels without knowing the primary level of social structure of the villagers or needy. The author assessed the situation within the four walls of the hospital in an exclusive manner without taking the family or society of the patient in consideration.

The study of Minocha[17] dealing in "Aspects of the social system of an Indian hospital" was an attempt to find out the social system of hospital which is a part of the macro-system of the society, without going into the various interacting components of macro-system of which hospital is a part. The study also ignores the gradual growth of modern hospital, which grew out of the very western ideology without being consentaneous to the culture of the people of the area.

In the study of "Doctors and Nurses" by Oommen,[18] issues, like inter strata rivalry with in the four walls of the hospital and the legtimisation of status of each stratum raised, particularly incase of the nurses, thereby raising the question of professionalism versus semi-professionalism (doctors versus nurses).

The study of Madan,[19] "Doctors and Society" is an attempt to understand the super specialised institute, its genesis, guide line of work, staffing pattern, logistics, and the types of doctors working there and their socio-economic background and so forth.

Advani[20] in his "Doctor patient relationship in Indian hospital" has essentially gone into some old conceptual imbroglio of spacio-temporal limitations and wings and wards as well as logistics. The study deals with large range of Delhi hospitals, dealing with the size of the hospital, bed facilities, total staff strength. A scale of performance was designed in terms of performance of the hospitals in relation to their respective size and subsequently a correlation of inverse order was drawn. larger the hospital lesser the influence of the patient on the doctors. Even, it was found that doctors are happy to work in large hospital.

Statistical design of refined order were evolved to analyse the data collected but the actual issues remained untouched viz, the need of such varieties of hospitals, to what extent those have fulfilled the commitment of health care delivery for the needy, where does the patient fit into such kind of institutional health care maze.

In a similar, study by the same scholar entitled, "Dimension of patient satisfaction", he has gone into the issues of patients satisfaction within the given structure of the hospital. The study remained confined in the strapping of Western model of patient health care and his sick role performance analysis. But, the need of the hour is to see the phenomena in a larger perspective of the overall social system and culture.

A study carried out by Venkataratnam[21] "Medical Sociology in an Indian setting", conducted in two different hospitals of Madras has gone into the doctor, nurse role, in terms of their own perception, role expectation and actual role performance of their own roles, dissatisfaction or satisfaction due to performance of expected roles and the causes thereof.

And finally, finding out the Sociological status of role interaction that emerges out from an analysis of role performance in a hospital. Such studies by and large become intellectual discourse of sociological facts rather than finding or helping to find out the real sociological issues in patient care in the overall institutional health care system. There is an urgency to make the role of doctors more (patients) need centric in order to make the system more functional and meaningful.

A study carried out by Chandani,[22] "A sociological study of doctors of Jodhpur city." Doctors class and caste background were observed in detail but failed to go into the complexities which are acting as confounding factors in the health care system.

The series of studies mentioned above have applied cosmetic redressal in the understanding of socio-cultural dimensions of clinically oriented health care system of this country. A major issue had been always overlooked in hospital studies that, it is not the ultimate in health care rather it is a part of the overall social system. By ignoring this fact any number of study in and around hospital would look to be a cosmetic redressal to a malignant issue, which is a lesser comprehensive assessment of the situation.

Institutional health care studies in the west those made impact and influenced the Indian scholars the following are prominent.

Primarily, the sick role performance in the hospitals of an inmate and the affective neutrality of the doctor while treating the patient (Parson 1951).[23] Parsonian study has dealt the patients of such cultural background, who are oriented in a health care system governed by the law of the institution but not by an individuals socio-cultural values or custom oriented, on the contrary the western patients are oriented to a high degree of cause and effect oriented values and paractices even while dealing with their own health and illness.

The studies of Tuckett[24] and Mechanic[25] on "Medical Sociology", dealt hospital as a complex organisation of health care delivery with specific roles defined for each staff inclusive of patients. The concept of job specificity, management of logistics and optimisation of administrative functions in hospital were discussed in their study. Szaz[26] and Hollander in their "A contribution to the philosophy of medicine", have primarily dealt with the basic models of the doctor patient relationship, besides the interstaff relationships more in the light of organisation rather than assessing the role performance, behaviour and expectations in a greater socio-cultural milieu. Their study is by and large an extension of Parsonian role performance model.

"The Hospital in Modern Society" of Friedson[27] has dealt the specialist wards and advanced technology real situation in the wards and how the services are being optimised. The role and status of each cadre — The therapeutic advancement and patients cooperation to carry out the technical excellence were discussed in detail.

An Alternative Approach

Another school of thought evolved in contradiction to above group of thinkers, trying to define health as a broader phenomena rather than illness or disease. And laid emphasis to the fact that the institutional health care needs to be seen in a holistic manner to encompass all the components having direct or indirect bearing on health.

The studies of these groups of workers were concerned with the health care in much more broader perspective. More community based approaches were taken up, by those scholars, hospital is not at the helm of the overall system, rather it is a sub-system of the overall system (basic plank of those studies). According to Sahu[28] "medicine's failure to develop a positive definition of health results from the individualistic and ideological bias that pervades medical research and medical practice, structures relations between practitioners and patients shapes the approaches selected for treatment (e.g. chemical or surgical intervention) and the technology employed and rejects and initiation of collective social action by communities."

Further, Sahu adds that health care is not merely hospital bound technologically oriented exercise but health services are one of the main factors influencing the health status of a population. Health of a population is also influenced, by social, economic factors as well as factors like nutrition, housing, education, income and its distribution, employment, communication and transportation and the social structure. Moreover, as the other factors influencing the health status, the health services of a community is usually a function of its political system. Political forces play a dominant role in shaping the health services of the community through decisions on resource allocations, manpower policy, choice of technology and also the degree to which the health services are to be available and accessible to the population.

Furthermore, according to Sahu some social planners while exploring the causes of backwardness of society, have pointed out the mutually potentiating influence of the major social problems of hunger, unemployment, illiteracy, denial of social justice, poor sanitation, sickness and general insensitivity towards stimuli for change. Health status of a country is thus intimately linked with other social and economic conditions. People are sick because they are poor, they become poorer because they are sick and consequently sick becomes poorer, and ultimately that leads to a vicious circle. The entire spectrum of such interdependency and its subsequent effect on health has been well understood by Banerji[29] in the light of "health culture." It defines, "the cultural meaning of health problems and the means it adopts for dealing with them both in terms of formation of various health institutions and the health behaviour or of individuals or of groups". In the same light Banerji further argues, "because of its cultural connotation, health culture undergoes change with in the overall culture as a result of cultural innovations and cultural diffusion. It may also change as a result of purposive intervention from outside aimed at bringing about a desired change. Conversely, any change within the health culture of society has repercussions on its overall culture".

Similarly, studies by Ivan Illich has highlighted the over technicalised, mystified medicine of today which needs a stock taking, mere accumulation of hardwares in health care and extreme commercialisation, according to him, is a nemesis to the system. Illich has strongly raised voice against extensive iatrogenesis, high degree of professionalisation leading to a formation of hiatus between larger mass and the institute, centralisation which leads to concentration of power, facility and resource gets accumulated at one point only, on the contrary he emphasised for "peoples health in peoples hand" or a larger degree of community participation. And he is also against mystification of medicine. Demystification is essential in order to make the system more accessible, affordable and available for the people.

Antia[30], has dealt the health and health care in a holistic dimension as he states, "we continue to follow the increasing sophisticated western model of illness care, although, the affluent countries in the west are themselves finding it increasingly difficult to meet the cost of such services and have started questioning its rationality." He further went on to say, "it must be realised that these countries during last century have by a process of social economic and political development eliminated almost all the major causes of morality and morbidity that at present account for the vast majority of our health problems. Their present problems of health and their pattern of disease have little in common with ours where the low health status cause lies mainly in poverty and not in affluence except in the cause of minority of our urban elite. Our problems are predominantly of communicable diseases not of cancer, stroke, heart disease or automobile accidents...". Antia further went on describing that........ "Yet our medical profession brought up under the spell of western medicine and dictated by a market economy is chiefly interested in catering to a small affluent and influential segment of our society whose needs are more akin to those of the west rather than those of the poor masses. All these things have led to distortion of priorities in health. The system is highly medicalised." The emphasis is on the sophisticated urban hospital based system with the neglect of the rural population and of the most elementary community services, even in urban slums the situation is no different. Antia also mentioned the improper imitation of the West in every sphere of hospital, dispensary or P.H.C. health care service has left people with no alternatives.

According to him, there is an urgency to reverse such abject situation by pluging the loopholes of the system.

Navarro's,[31] study of Chile has raised many issues of health care delivery of western type and the political economy of the drug market besides commercial exploitation by industrially developed nations of the west of that of the not so developed or under developed nations in one or the other pretext. Dumping of banned drugs from the advanced countries to not so advanced or less advanced nations and its consequences on the health care system of the poor people at large been dealt at length by Navarro.

Absolute commodification of health care delivery system, has created conditions in which health of human being has been reduced to a mere commodity, which is weighed in the light of profit and loss, capital invested and gains accrued there of, highlighting the greed of a bunch of disguised medical do gooders.

Djurfeldt and Lindberg[32] in the study of the introduction of Western Medicine in a Tamil village has gone into great details to know the level of appreciation of indigenous medical practices versus western medicine. The study entitted "Pills against Poverty" has successfully drawn sharp distinction in the various types of practices in the village in terms of faith healing approach. popularity based treatment. They have emphasised the "shortsightedness of health policy which spends its meager resources on one medical system which provides only part of medical services while the other systems which are equally important as that of the allopathic are left unsupervised, undetected and unfinanced so that they slowly degenerate and decay." (Pills against Poverty, 1975).

The study of Djurfeldt and Lindberg categorically mentioned certain parameters which are impeding any progress of the western medical system i.e. under utilisation of the medical facilities, the irrational use of resources, the emphasis is on cure rather than prevention. the general structure of the society in which the modern allopathic medical system is supposed to function is by and large non receptive to its practice. Also, because it can do little to alleviate the result of abject poverty, malnutrition and deficiencies in hygiene and sanitation. Consequently, "the relative inefficiency of the allopathic system is the basic reason for the relative efficiency of the indigenous system" (Djurfeldt and Lindberg). And, finally they said health problems are not only technical or political or economic alone but also socio-cultural in nature.

According to Zurbrigg,[33] paradox of urban setting is, too many doctors but still there is gap between the rich and the poor in terms of health care even in the cities. Besides, the study has also stressed on the whims and fancies of the doctors for poor patients admission in the hospital or for that matter into the main fold of health care. Moreover, the admission to hospital of the patient is highly determined by the private visits patient makes to doctor at his clinic. It was also stressed that the exclusion of the poor from the health care market is based on affordability. The ability to pay is very important as majority of the doctors are in private practice.

According to, Chatterjee in the existing model the doctor is in the centre with all others are in the periphery. And, there exists interaction, amongst doctor, bureaucrat, politician but for community, which has no access to doctors. To modify the system, community should be considered into centre of relations. Directives should reach to others from the community. And a link should exist between community and health care institute.

The need to carry out this study was felt necessary as most of the scholars touched the issues of health and health care in a non holistic fashion.

Moreover, to understand the slum health situation certain factors need to be looked into, those can make the understanding of the problem more lucid and can help evolve a much more accountable and comprehensive system of health care delivery. To look into the various impedements in the delivery system one has to understand the following issues after fine tooth comb.

- To study hospital in the context of delivery of health care services to the slum or resettlement is appropriate under such circumstances when net growth of logistics and hardware are taking place in cities and the slum or resettlement colony people are still suffering equally, if not more, than the villagers. The plight of urban slum (health) more or less remained unchanged in majority of the case.

- The exponential growth of public and private sector hospitals and dispensaries in the cities are serving to which group or class, becomes a key question to be answered. So, the obvious query in ones mind floats high is to what extent the people of periphery are being served and are they satisfied with the services, they aregetting.

- Last but not the least the study of urban slums health care is long due and so far almost no effort has been made in this direction. In order to initiate the same the present study and discourse has been formulated.

Slum: A Life Style in Urban India

It has been estimated by experts of town planning and city development, besides, the economists and other social scientist that one third of worlds population live in sub-standard housing conditions in urban areas and this situation is likely to worsen in the years to come.

At present, there are over two lakh squatter families with population of ten to eighteen lakh (as the people are not stable-the population varies) and there are more than five hundred unauthorised colonies dotting all over India. Out of one crore population of Delhi nearly fifty five lakhs (55%) live in unauthorised colonies, notified slums, planned/developed resettlement colonies and Jhuggi Jhopri clusters.[31]

The slum has been defined by UNESCO as... "a slum is a building, a group of buildings or area characterised by over crowding deterioration, unsanitary conditions or absence of facilities or any one of them endanger the health safety of its inhabitants of the community." Given the above definition of slum, a segmented study of one aspect of slum i.e. social structure, housing pattern, sanitation and hygiene or any other social institution is incomplete effort to know a slum. To understand the slum comprehensively, there is a necessity to understand the phenomena in its broader perspective.

So far many scholars of different social science stream namely, sociology, economics, anthropology and political science have carried out the studies in various parts of the world as well as in India on slums. Most of the studies attempted to look into slum problems in only two major dimensions.

1. It is a rural urban continuum.
2. It is a distinct sub-cultural group within a larger socio-cultural milieu. Or in other words, an independent phenomena.

The famous study of Lewis[35] on rural urban continuum has given a vivid description of the legacy of the rural custom and culture reflecting upon the activities of the peripheral urban squatter in their day to day life process.

The squatters been also called as "buffer zone" between the city and the village. All these studies have shown the underlying link or an umbilical connection with folk society of the urban slums, studies on these lines have also been carried out in India. The Hindu social institution and its perpetuation in an urban setting has been described in the article of Raj Gandhi,[36] entitled "Social Structure of Urban India, Continuities and Changes." Other scholars i.e. Brush,[37] studied, "Eighty Indian Cities and the Social Structure." Bose,[38] "Calcutta: A Social Survey", Gist,[39] Mehta and Hazelhurst "The Morphology of Indian Cities", all these studies highlited maintenance of fibres of Hindu social structure in a different (non rural) setting. It is quite smooth and remains undaunted inspite of internal and external forces of stress and strain generated by the ever chaing politico-economic sphere of slum or resettlement. Though, a group of scholars have given hypothesis to defy the above school of thought. The caste group gives rise to class in urban setting has predominated many studies. But one wonders that the studies never emphasised the status and situation of urban slum in the context of health which is an undefiable reality.

Many scholars have been studying the urban development of Indian society in the light of little tradition and greater tradition of Redfield[40] (study conducted on Yucatans in Mexico). This was emulated in India by Singer[41] and Marriott[42] in U.P in the village of (Kisangarhi). The concept of modernisation and Sanskritisation of M.N. Srinivas[43] have helped to understand the city or urban life and its dynamics of change. Lesser mortals of the Hindu society attaining a higher place in his own sub societal group and thereby acquiring power to chattange Brahminical authority and hierarchy in the caste ladder.

The slum is an outgrowth, it is the by-product of massive urbanisation and capitalist development. Above concept of development has worked strongly in growth of one of the most finest cities of West Europe and can be explained in the words of E. Engles[44]...... "The main solution of slum problem sought after in the capitalist world was first introduced in Paris. It was here that Haussmann flourished as town planner, the first bourgeois modern town planner who reconstructed Paris. He destroyed for more than a tangle of slums and thieves kitchen. He did much more than to eliminate and scatter the working population to the four corners of the city of Paris and out to the farthest suburb. He destroyed the very image evoked by the former working class districts by not only reconstructing them altogether but even changing their names, he designated the common working masses of Paris as the mob, the vagabonds and nomads."

This strategy of clearing the slums continue even to this day in many of our cities as well. In one of the "Sardar Patel Memorial Lectures",1983. Mr. Jagmohan[45] the former Chairman of Delhi Development Authority while talking on, "The challenge of our cities", justified the slum clearance of 1975 in Delhi and there after spreading them in the out skirts of Delhi. In his lecture he once said in anguish, "our cities have slums primarily because the power to clean or prevent them has been taken away from us."

Some studies carried out in Indian slums have dealt the dimensions of political consciousness and affiliation to the various religious cum political groups with the slum i.e. "A womans encounter of Arya Samaj and untouchables : A slum in Jullendur" by Dua.[46] Another study was carried out in almost in the same fashion in Kanpur, of the slum, of textile mill workers by Bellwinkell.[47] One study was carried out by D. Varadachari[48] in the slums of Madras where the scholars have seen the social life, interaction and, social mobility amongst the members of the slum.

A review of Indian slum situation was carried by Hiremath[49] in his "India's Urban Slum", where he has concluded by saying, "Let us commence with cleanliness activity in our slums. With this, it is relatively easier to improve our slums than otherwise we have to start with most humble programme of keeping our cities clean. Slum improvement does not imply creation of more slums, (p. 81)." Slum improvement can not be taken up in isolation. To improve slum one has to improve other components which are directly or indirectly affecting slum"....

Another study carried out by Pillai,[50] "Slum the nature and the extent of problem in India," has revealed that Indian slums have maluntrition, unsanitary and poor conditions, crime, indebtedness, prostitution, unemployment and general poverty. He has also mentioned the multiplier affect of slum growth in all the Indian cities. Besides, described in general the growth of Bombay slum (in an exponential manner) and its various ever lasting problems.

It is clear from the above mentioned studies that the scholars have dealt urbanisation and subsequently slum growth in the light of the political structure and various social institutions, gangsterism, the poor sanitation and hygiene but a very few has talked of over all health situation in slum. A study was carried out in Calcutta metropolis with emphasis on the under developed area (by city standard) in Beleghata as well as in Chetla by Banerji et al., to find out the status and condition of living of the slum dwellers with particular emphasis on the health status. The scholars found that the health, hygiene and sanitation have improved relatively in late eighties than what it was in mid-seventies. Some of these developments are attributable to state intervention and political will of the ruling party in West Bengal.

Another study carried out by Klein[51] titled "Calcutta a metropolis; with emphasis on the slum or under developed area" has portrayed that in the late nineteenth century and early twentieth century the development of the city was compounded with high disease and mortality rate. The high rate of morality in Calcutta bustees or other areas were due to material development and its effect in causing environmental problems and nullifying the benefits of public health measures, so the mortality was not due to plague or famine.

He also said that the over crowding, bad housing high cost of living and primacy of laissez-faire market in urban development posed threat to human life. So, the officials cleared slums. And modified the tap water system and renewed the urban set up but that too paid a very small dividend. The private speculators became stronger and stronger, at the cost of the gradual growth (unbriddled in nature) of housing societies and buildings, they made their profit and flourished as strong and powerful economic strata of the society. And such situation combined with political unwillingness to provide sound urban health or reluctance to assess the distribution of social benefits to the poor led to such bizarre health situation in the city of Calcutta and other state townships.

A study carried out in Patna slum by a team of scholars Sinha,[52] Singh and Karn in 1987 found the following facts. It is an appalling situation, it is a breeding ground of germs. The city is full of garbage littered around the stray cattles are moving around in all directions without any check. The individuals of slum keep their surroundings clean at their own cost. The study also described the low literacy rate combined with poor economy of slum dwellers and need to improve the overall situation.

The need is to provide them with illness cure, health care amenities, removal of child labour. There is a necessity to improve their earning capacity. There is need to provide them with opportunities for good health and health care facility. A better type of rehabilitation is the need of the hour but mere demolition of slums is no answer to this problem.

Many studies have been carried out in Bombay slums, the studies on Bombay slums have been carried out by scholars like Desai and Pillai[53] in 1970. And by Ramchandran in 1972 and of late a team of government officials of Bombay and university of Edinburgh carried out a study on the health status of the Dharavi children in 1985.

The earlier studies have gone into the detailed-mechanics of slum formation in Bombay and the contemporary socio-cultural and economic status of the slums. It was revealed in every study that heavy industrialisation led to slum formation in Bombay particularly the textile mills of nineteenth and early twentieth century brought in unskilled and skilled people from Ratnagiri, Satara, Thane to Bombay and with the passage of time those Chawls (single room tenement of mill residents) became over-crowded and were no less than slums.

The Dharavi study on preschool children (1985)[54] showed children suffered of gastroenteritis, T.B., respiratory tract infection, worm infection, skin infection and many other minor ailments. It was also found with each infection the child gets nutritionally depleted ultimately result in slow growth and loss of weight. The knowledge of Oral Rehydration Theraphy (ORT) was not common amongst the mothers. Most of the time children were given infected foods in wrong manner (time and way of delivery). Thirty percent of ladies delivered low birth weight babies. Food supplementation started very late as well as slowly. Nutritional status of boys were relatively better than girls. ICDS programme started late in Dharavi so no results were found during the study, education to mothers were given to maintain child health and motivation against commercial milk. The study also recommended that there is a need to pressurise the authorities to change the situation in Dharavi, lock stock and barrel.

Similarly, a study carried out in Delhi by National Institute of Health and Family Welfare[55] in 1986 revealed interesting facts. The study was carried out in three slums and one resettlement colony of Delhi. It was felt by the group that the existing health care strategy for the slum health care in Delhi was not adequate. It was reinforced by the studies carried out in three different slums. It was found in Mangolpuri (resettlement) conflict situation was prevailing amongst the people of the area, the government functionaries and the political leaders. The conflict was contingent upon the quality of health care dispensed to the people in that area. The welfare programmes did not reach upto the people. ICDS was not functioning properly. There were shortage of medicine and vaccine in local dispensaries. Schools did not function properly. There was a demand of all round better civic amenities including the health care facilities.

Seelampur, another Janata Majdoor colony studied by the team showed that no infighting existed amongst the people and functionaries, people were relatively well off in economic sense. But the need of civic amenities were utmost in the residents minds. Jhuggi Jhopri colony of Nehru Place inhabited by construction labours was another slum area studied by the same team and they found that the area lacked minimum hyiegenic standard of living. No facilities were given to the construction workers. The improper defecation spots created problem for the labourers, the passer by and the residents of adjoining area. There was no day care centre for children. The vulnerable age group and women were exposed to all health hazards of construction.

They also studied Ballimaran a highly congested urban conglomerate of old Delhi. As per the study it has been stated that the area being congested with density of 250 person per acre, there was a chance of spread of diseases in an epidemic form. The interview carried out in this area amongst the local leaders who were mostly the doctors, teachers and shopkeepers did not mention of any particulars need for the colony. Few problems were mentioned by them, such as, need of milk booth, need of post office and provision for mid-day meal for the children. However, a small fraction wanted more health care and education facilities.

The studies mentioned above showed the people of resettlement or slum are living a life of appaling misery in most of the cases.

The slums and resettlements dué to their very typical nature deserve a greater deal of attention to be paid and there is a need to study these sttlements with their available health care facilities. The studies reiterated the need to study the health culture of the resettlers in the context of available and accessible hospital services. However, a group of thinkers believes the development of the slum and the poor can be had by making them the instrument of the process. People are the resource for development; their own energies and creative intelligence and intent. They are more important than government aids, experties or social agencies efforts. The basis of their hypothesis is people must become the subjects of the verb of development, not the objects. The doers, not the done for.

NOTES

1. Bhore, J. *et al., National Health Survey and Development Committee*, G.O.I, Vol-(I-IV) 1946.
2. Mudaliar, A., *National Health Survey and Planning Committee*, G.O.I, Vol-(I&II), 1962.
3. Singh, K., *Report on the Committee on MPW*, Ministry of Health and Family Welfare, 1973.
4. Shrivastava, *Group on Medical Education and Support Manpower*, 1975.
5. ICMR & ICSSR , *Health for All : An Alternative Strategy*, ICMR,1981.
6. National Health Policy, *Statements on National Health Policy*, Ministry of Health & Family Welfare (1982 a).
7. Illich, I., *Limits to Medical Nemes is : The Expropriation of Health*,1975.
8. *Ibid.*
9. Jeffery, R., *Medical Policy making in India in the 1970. Out of Dependency*, 1980.
10. Chatterjee, M., *Implementing Health Policy*, 1988.
11. De Almedia Francisco, *Portugese Commander Came to India* in 1506.
12. Megaw, R.K., 1938, London, U.K.
13. Pocket Book of Health Statistics, Ministry of Health &Family Welfare, Govt. of India, New Delhi, 1983.
14. Mathur, I., *Human Organisation of a Hospital*, 1975.
15. Parson and Fox, *Excerpt from Talcott Parsons the Structure of Social Action*, 1952.
16. Krikpatrick, J., *The Delivery of Hospital Services in North India*, Punjab, Ludhian. *A Client Institution Interaction Model*, pp. 125-48, 1981.
17. Minocha, A., *Some Aspects of the Social System of an Indian Hospital*, 1974.

18. Oommen, T.K., *Doctors and Nurses,* 1978.
19. Madan, T.N., *Doctors and Society,* 1980.
20. Advani, M., *Doctor Patient Relationship in India Hospital,* 1980.
21. Venkataratnam, R., *Medical Sociology in an Indian Setting,* 1979.
22. Chandani., A. *A Sociological Study of Doctors of Jodhpur City,* 1987.
23. Parson, T., *The Structure of Social Action* 1952.
24. Tuckett, D., *Medical Sociology,* 1978.
25. Mechanic, D., *Medical Sociology,* 1978.
26. Szaz, T., *A Contribution to the Philosophy of Medicine.*
27. Friedson, E., *Profession of Medicine: A study of Sociology of Applied Knowledge,* 1970.
28. Sahu, S.K., *Health Culture of Orgons of Rourkela and Hinterland,* J.N.U, Ph.D. Thesis, 1980.
29. Banerji, D., *Poverty Class and Health Culture,* 1982.
30. Antia, N.H., "Big Hospitals for Whose Benefit", *Indian Express,* 6th June; 1988.
31. Navaro, V., *Allendes Chile: A Case Study in the Breaking of Under-development Medicine under Capitalism,* 1976.
32. Djurfeldt, G. and Lindberg, S., *Pills against Poverty: A study of the Introduction of Western Medicine in Tamil Village,* 1975.
33. Zurbrigg, S., *Rakku's soory: Structure of Ill Health and Source of Change* 1984, pp-83-84.
34. Delhi Development Authority, *A Report of the Chairman,* New Delhi; 1984.
35. Lewis, O., *La Vida: A Puertarican Family in Culture of Poverty;* San Juan and New York, 1976.
36. Gandhi, R., *Social Structure of Urban India: continuities and changes.*
37. Brush, J.E., *Indian Cities and Social Structure.*
38. Bose, N.K., *Calcutta: A Social Survey.*
39. Gist, N.P., (*et. al.*), *The Morphology of Indian Cities.*
40. Redfield, R., "The Social Organisation of Tradition" *Far Eastern Quarterly,* vol. 15, pp. 1955-56.
41. Singer, M., "The Great Tradition in Metropolitan Centre: Madras", *Traditional India,* p. 141.
42. Marriott, M., *Social Structure and Change in a U.P. Village* (ed), M.N. Srinivas; 1955.
43. Srinivas, M.N., The Social Structure of a Mysore Village"; *India's Villages,* 1966.
44. Engles, F., *The Housing Question Marx-Engle Selected Work,*Vol. II.
45. Jagmohan, *Sardar Patel Memorial Lecture.* New Delhi, 1983.
46. Dua, V., *A Womans Encounter of Arya Samaj and Untouchable: A Sulm in Jullendur.*
47. Bellwinkell, M., *A study on Slums of Textile Mill Workers in Kanpur.*
48. Vardachari, B.D., *Slums of Madras City.*
49. Hiremath, S.G., *India's Urban Slum.*

50. Pillai, S.D., *Slum the Nature and the Extent of Problem in India.*
51. Klein, I., *Calcutta Metropolis: with Emphasis on the Slum or Under Developed Area.*
52. Sinha, G.P. (et. al). *A Study of Patna Slum Paper Presented in Seminar.* New Delhi, 1987.
53. Desai, A.R. & Pillai S.D. (Ed.), *A Profile of an Indian Slum:* Asia Publishing House, Bombay.
54. UNICEF & TISS, *A Study of Dharavi Slums*, Bombay, 1985.
55. NIHFW; *A Study of Health Statutus of Delhi Slums*, Delhi, 1986.

2

RESETTLEMENT AND ITS GENESIS

Evolution of Resettlement Colony in Delhi

In the light of overall slum development in India, Delhi's share is no less, Mr. Jagmohan erstwhile Chairman, Delhi Development Authority, wrote in 1979: "a recent study of the squatter settlements in Delhi by Town and Country Planning Organisation, reveals that more than half a million people are living in 1373 clusters of Jhuggi Jhopri".[1] It also indicates that "whereas in 1951 these were only one 'squatter' household over 20 non squatter households in urban Delhi, it was so in 1973 for less than 5 non-squatter households. Besides, this the squatter population has been growing at the annual rate of 12 per cent in comparison to the city's 4.5 percent".[2]

The scheme of slum clearance was in operation in Delhi in the notified slum areas of walled city and its extensions since 1956. Under this programme, dangerous/dilapidated buildings and pockets notified as clearance areas under slum areas (Improvement and Clearance) act 1956 were cleared and families affected by unavoidable clearance operations launched due to the fact that areas/building/properties becoming unfit for residential purposes, had been rehabilitated in flats constructed in slum resettlement in different parts of Delhi. Under slum clearance scheme, various changes were brought in form time to time since 1956 till 1975.[3]

National emergency of 1975 brought in many changes in the topography of Delhi along with the country under the operation of "clearance and beautification of Delhi", all the unauthorised slum, shanties and squatter colonies were cleared and bulldozed. These squatters were spread all over Delhi. As they had occupied Delhi Development Authorities (DDA) earmarked woodland plots, plots for private housing and few of them encroached the road side pavements and huge sewage pipes, it was felt by the state that these were to be removed from the city, lock stock and barrel. Moreover, those colonies which came up without any permission, of Delhi Development Authority i.e. various post partition refugees hutments of Kingsway Camp, Vijay Nagar in North Delhi, Turkman Gate in Central Delhi, Krishna Nagar, Arjun Nagar of South Delhi. Some colonies of the West Delhi near Tilak Nagar to be face lifted for a better and cleaner Delhi. Although, these rsettlements came up long ago in 1947-48, over a period of time with the implementation of original master plan of Delhi, it became a necessity, to demolish these colonies and were reallocated at quite high price to the housing societies where flats were made and sold at good premium. And evicted people became landless evacuees and many of them resigned to their faith and became floater. It must be noted that two categories of displaced persons came up due to the cleaning operation.

The first category of evacuees were those, who were shanty dwellers and evicted from their temporary dwellings (These are the people who are mostly labourers in unorganised sector, people running their own petty shops or working as domestic helps).

The second category were those who were the post partition refugees who were settled in various parts of Delhi in barracks and hutments also became homeless once again due to city clearing plan of post emergency.

The latter group could manage a better places of resettlement and good site in the colony by:

- Encashing their contact, which they built over years.
- By giving money as bribe wherever they could afford to give.
- By remaining united and representing to authorities and ultimately convincing them, (whereas the former group could not do any such arrangement) to allot better plots to these peoples.

Resettlement: A Mode of Slum Rehabilitation

With promulgation of national emergency in the year 1975, it was decided by Delhi Administration and other public bodies that all the squatter and slum colonies of the capital were be cleared and in turn resettlement colonies to be built. By 1976, almost all the resettlement colonies were allotted to the slum or Jhuggi dwellers. Most of the resettlement colonies were agricultural or farm land in the outskirts of the city. The resettlement colonies came up in North, East, West and South Delhi. Delhi Development Authority procured the lands at Rs. 5 to Rs. 8 per square yard. Each household was given a cut out of 25 square yards, and all the colonies were leased for 99 years. The resettlement was done with certain specific objectives, in mind.

A decent living for the slum dwellers by providing them at namely, least minimum provision of basic civic amenities i.e. clean water supply, sanitary tank or water sealed latrine, electricity, park and lawn for children to play, metalled roads and proper drainage system.

In later years, it was thought that the resettlement of slum colonies should be a concept by which one should get "Shelter (to live) and Site" (to earn livelihood) together.

The provision of school, health facilities i.e. dispensaries, hospital run by government or corporation or allied bodies was also envisaged.

The houses were built with certain scientific understanding so that in small area with least cost input maximum facilities could be provided but in that process a lot of compromises were done with living space and ventilation facilities. And the shortage of space forced the dwellers to avil community latrine facilities, of late the houses in some of the resettlement colonies been provided by domestic tap water supply and w/c laterine.

The resettlement colonies were built in 1975-76 and were constructed till 1985. Thereafter the plan and construction of resettlement colonies were abandoned, as it became conspicious and obvious that the programme was an unviable exercise to accomodate teeming million who were scattered all over the city. In the span of ten years, the Delhi Development Authority constructed forty-five resettlement colonies.

The resettlement colonies house nearly 3 million people. It has been reported by Delhi Development Authority that today 5 million or 50% of Delhi's population live in slums. According to above mentioned sources 1.5 million people live in Jhuggi, Jhopries, 2.0 million in slum designated area: Shajahanabad (ward 1 to ward 17) Chandersekhar Azad Colony (near Gulabi Bagh), parts of Pahar Ganj, Nabi Karim, Navjeewan camp (opposite to Kalkaji), Tigri near Khanpur Depot, Zafrabad (Janta Mazdoor colony), Lal Bagh, Raghubir Nagar (near Najafgard). (Delhi Development Authority: Slum Wing Report 1989).

Table: 2.1
Distribution of Resettlement Colonies of Delhi
(Source : D.D.A. Slum wing)

Sl.No.	*East*	*West*	*North*	*South*
1	Seelampur Ph-I, II, III, IV	Najafgarh Road Sector-A, D, E&G, F	Mangolpuri Ph-I,	Sunlight Colony
2.	Seelampur Additional Ph-II Plot	Hastasal	Mangolpuri	Srinivas Puri
3.	Seelampur old	Madipur	Mangolpuri Ph-III	Garhi village
4.	Seelampur New Ph-I, II, III	Nangloi Ph-I, II, III, IV, V	Sultanpuri Additional Plot	Kalkaji
5.	Patparganj complex Plot	Wazirpur	Sultanpuri Additional	Madangiri
6.	Trilokpuri	Shakurpur Ph-IV	Jahangirpuri	Dakshinpuri
7.	Kalyanpuri	Shakurpur Ph-III	--	Dakshinpuri extn.
8.	Kichripuri	Shakurpur Ph-I and II	Kondli	Tigri
9.	Nand Nagari	Khyala Ph-I Ph-I, II, III	Nehru Vihar	Moti Bagh
10.	Nand Nagari Ph-II	Gokulpuri	Wazirpur	Pandu Nagar
11.	Nand Nagari	Chankhandi	--	Ranjit Nagar
12.	--	--	--	Naraina
13.	--	--	--	Inderpuri J.J. Colony, Manglapuri

Although, for all official and administrative purpose since 1985, the resettlement colonies have been reconsidered as slum. The resettlement colonies were built in such a way that maximum number of people could be housed in minimum possible area. Most of the people in these colonies are engaged in unorganised sectors or they are self employed as well as few of them are daily wage earners, wheeler dealer. Most of the migrant population of these colonies came from adjoining sates of Delhi at different point of time in various phases. And settled in Jhuggi, Jhopries or in resettlement colonies.

The inhabitants of resettlement colony of Delhi were found to be from different cultural background because they were from different states i.e. Haryana, Rajasthan, Uttar Pradesh, Bihar, Tamil Nadu and West Bangal. They came in search of their livelihood in Delhi. During their stay in slums, they were exposed to various onslaughts, such onslaughts are the manifestations of rapid and indiscreet urbanisation of the capital city. Lot of changes were seen in their day to day life processes. These changes have been negotiated by these people to cope up with urgent felt need faced, by the dwellers. Such an adaptability came handy to deal with other cultural groups.

In general, the culture of any community is the key component to understand the health culture and its dynamics.

The culture study is a part of an effort made to assess the health culture of the inhabitants of the resettlement colony and the people staying near the resettlement colony. As the inherent health care institutions and their services shapes up the health culture of the community the emphasis been given to understand how far the available health care facilities have influenced the present health culture of the people.

The Study

The present study has gone into the following objectives:

(a) To understand the life process of the people of resettlement colony (which is supposed to provide a better life chance to the slum dwellers of Delhi).

(b) To study how far the inhabitants of resettlement colony placed in the outskirts of the city have got the access to wide range of health care facilities which are available in different hospitals of the city.

(c) Finally, an attempt been made to examine how the present health culture of the resettlers in Delhi have evolved against the backdrop of the socio-economic life process of resettlement *vis-a-vis* the various existing institutional health care services.

Jahangirpuri was found to be the oldest of the forty five resettlement established by DDA. The colony happened to be characteristically representative of the forty five resettlement colonies. As a result, it provided ample scope to take up Jahangirpuri to represent the resettlement culture and health care status. This colony being the oldest of forty five. It retained various original entity of the rural setting as well as rural urban continuum in its true form.

Characteristics of the Resettlement of Jahangirpuri

- Jahangirpuri is one of the oldest resettlement colony.
- It is connected by motorable roads from all directions.
- It is well connected by public transportation i.e. Delhi Transportation Corporation buses ply from all corners of the city. The resettlers have easy accessibility to nearby hospitals (Government and missionary run).
- It is interesting to study as it provides an ideal rural urban continuum because it is flanked by 300 years old Bhalasawa village.
- Moreover, this colony and the adjoining village was easily accessible by the scholar. Besides, its greater density of population with high degree of heterogenity which provide a wide range of issues to study about the health and culture of the people residing there.

To understand the health culture of the resettlers, it was necessary to undertake a detailed study of the total life style of resettlers along with that of the villagers of Bhalasawa. The village is much more older and stabler entity than the colony of Jahangirpuri. Moreover, the people of Jahangirpuri and the village Bhalasawa constituted a wider cultural kaleidoscope. Which not only provided deep insight into the health culture but also gave an opportunity for an in-depth culture study.

In Jahangirpuri resettlement colony, six blocks were studied in detail out of ten blocks. The above table shows the selected households of the colony and the village as well.

Table : 2.2
Distribution of House Holds Covered in Different Blocks of Resettlement and Village Bhalaṣawa

S.No	*Village Blocks*	*Number of Plots*	*Covered Blocks and Household for the Study*
1.	A	1890	150
2.	B	1799	98
3.	C	1949	154
4.	D	1799	-
5.	E	2897	150
6.	G	2000	-
7.	H	2000	-
8.	I	2000	154
9.	J	2000	-
10.	K	2000	150
11.	Bhalasawa Village	300	150
	Grand Total		1006

According to DDA, in phase-l, seven blocks were built, i.e. A.B.C.D.E.G and H out of which four blocks were studied viz. A.B.C. and E. And in phase-II, there were three blocks. I. J and K. out of which two were studied viz, I and K. The basis of selection of blocks were:

(a) A and B blocks were selected due to proximity to main road of the colony.

(b) C block was selected because most of the Muslim migrants from Bangladesh and north Bangal were resettled there.

(c) E & EE blocks were selected because a missionary clinic was working there.

(d) I block was selected because majority of the trader migrants were resettled there.

(e) K block was selected for the physical proximity with village to assess the direct impact of the village on the resettlement.

The methodology was useful to understand the health culture of a resettled population. Given this conceptual framework an anthropological approach was adopted to know about the people in detail which not only gave the picture of entire resettlement community but also the politico-economic status as well as their health care status at the given point of time and in retrospect as well. Besides, understanding the actual health care behaviour of different strata of the population, i.e. rich, middle and poor income groups in response to various health problems and their perception regarding different state sponsored health care programmes in the field of communicable and non communicable diseases was studied and analised thread-bare. Besides, opinion of the resettlers on population control was also assessed.

The social structure, the economic structure, the power structure and socio-cultural changes were also studied in order to get a better insight into the health culture of the population.

The low lying landscape of the village with big ditches and open drains all around, combined with umpteen member of breeding ground of mosquitoes were very common sight. There were no metalled road within the village. There was one panchayat house in the village, which was constructed by contribution. It was observed that the elderly used it as a meeting and gossip point during normal days. The hobnob of political activities can be seen there during and after village elections. The village has no dispensary or hospital within its territory.

The People

Out of nearly 16000 households in Jahangirpuri and 300 households of the village, 1000 households were selected from the six blocks as well as from the village Bhalasawa at the initial stage. Further, the economic grouping of the poor, middle and the rich were done on the basis of the income of the family per month i.e., income upto Rs 4000, between Rs. 4001-8000 and Rs. 8000 and above respectively, such a stratification helped to understand the resettlers economic capacity in particular and the socio-cultural behaviour in general.

Selection of Health Institutions

Choice of the hospitals and health care institutions were made on the basis of physical proximity. As per the definition of health culture it has been emphasised that in order to understand the health culture systematically of any community, one has to take note of the available health institutions which belongs to the community in the form of indigenous (home remedy), folk and ethnic medicine practised in the community and the institutions of the western medicines and its practitioners available within the community to meet the unmet felt needs of health care.

To shart with the local health care institutions were selected for the purpose of understanding the pattern of local institutional health care and the role of these institutions as referral body for the nearby M.C.D runned hospitals. The role of private practitioners were equally important and so it was felt necessary to discuss various local issues related to health or otherwise with them.

The distribution of local dispensaries is given in the table below:

Table: 2.3

The Location of Dispensaries in Different Block of Resettlement

Blocks	*Types of local health care institution*	*Total Number*
A	1. Employee State Insurance Dispensary 2. M.C.D run Mother and Child Health (MCH) Dispensary.	2
B	Delhi Administration run General Dispensary	1
C	Delhi Administration run Polyclinic (where specialists sit).	1
D	(MCD) Municipal Corporation of Delhi run MCH Centre	1
E	Missionary (Catholic) run General Dispensary and T.B. clinic	1
J	MCD run Ayurvedic Clinic and Malaria Detection and Eradication Centre	1
G	Delhi Administration run Dispensary & Birth and Death Registration Centre	1

NOTES

1. Planning Commissions Report - *Sixth Five Year Plan.* 1981-85, Government of India, 1981.
2. Jagmohan., *Seminar ; Summary, Urbanisation Growth of Slums; Social Conflict and Environmental Hazards",* New Delhi, p.28, 1979.
3. Delhi Development Authority (Slum wing), *D.D.A., Slum Wing Report,* 1988, I.P. Estate, New Delhi.
4. Banerji, D., *Poverty, Class and Health culture,* Delhi, 1982.

3
PEOPLE AND CULTURE

Jahangirpuri : A Profile of a resettlement

Jahangirpuri is one of the forty five resettlement colonies of Delhi. This was built in 1975 and the occupation of the plots started by 1976. Situated in the Bhalasawa census block, located in northern most part of the city. It owes, its name from the then pond which was located in this part of the city during the reign of emperor Jahangir and was used by him for fishing. The fact is further reinforced by the dilapidated relics of small castle in the colony, which stands as a testimony of emperor's property.

To the west of Jahangirpuri runs G.T. Karnal Road (a highway leading to Punjab & Haryana). In the east and north east of the colony, there lies village Bhalasawa which is three hundred years old. In the east, there is bye pass/outer ring road which also guards the colony and the village from the threat of flood (as, it was inundated by flood in the year of 1978). In the south, there lies a middle class colony which is known as Adarsh Nagar. This colony was under the jurisdiction of Delhi Development Authority till 31st May 1988, with certain changes in policy, the colony was handed over to Municipal Corporation of Delhi since 1st June 1988. This colony was made out of the land procured from the Bhalasawa village.

It spreads over an area of 480 hectares. This land was used exclusively for the purpose of farming and agriculture by the villagers. It was procured at a rate of Rs. 8/- per square yard from the villagers. This was a low lying area which was eight feet below the mean sea level. This was later levelled and developed by dumping waste and garbage brought from other parts of the city. Although, the adjoining fallow land is still low lying and it belongs to the villagers and used for the purpose of cattle grazing.

The colony is leased with government for 99 years the adjoining colonies are "free hold" and enjoys lot of administrative freedom. The colony was designed to house roughly fifteen thousand and five hundred families. Each plot was initially 25 square yard which was later made into 23 square yard. The deduction was made to make the roads and lanes for the colony.

Almost every row has 100 houses or a pair of 50 houses across each road. The backside of one is touching the back of the other. The colony is mainly divided into ten different blocks namely, A, B, C, D, E, G, H, I, J and K. The colony is mainly divided into two major phases, one half is on the north and the other is on the south as per DDA's specifications. In the north, there is I, J, K and in the south, there is A, B, C, D, E, divided by a 26 metter wide road and another motor road which is 9 meter wide, further it separates G and H from the above mentioned in the south.

Every block has small marketing complex where domestic goods as well as items of daily usage are sold. Besides, the local vendors of fruits and vegetables supply of other daily usage items can be had at the doorstep. Every block has designated area for park and lawn. Today ninety percent of these were not being maintained and have become dumping grounds of garbage.

The income, caste and religious group of the six blocks and the village have been given in Table 3.1 (a).

Seven blocks (A,B,C,D,E,H,J), have health care institutions of various types runned as well as administered by various administrative bodies of the city. And almost every block has around 15 practitioners practising various sorts of medicine i.e. Allopathic, Ayurvedic, Unani and mix of all kinds of system of medicine. The adjoining village of Bhalasawa has a bone-setter who is approached by many of the resettlement colony dwellers (if, any body gets sprain or fractures, his bone is set by him in his own way).

The distribution of plots and block are given in Table 3.1 (b). (Number of households covered in preliminary survey is also given).

Demographic Overview

So far as the occupancy of the colony is concerned, out of 20503 plots 15094 are occupied as per the records of DDA slum

Table: 3.1(a)

The Selected Households on the Basis of Income, Caste and Religious Groups of the Study Area

Block & Village	Total House-hold Covered	Income Groupings			Hindu								Religious Groups			
		Rich	Middle	Poor	Brahmins	Kashitriya	Kayastha	Vaisya	Yadav	Jat	SC	Total	Muslim	Christian	Sikh Jain	Other
Block-A	150	35	72	43	9	62	3	33	-	-	18	125	-	-	25	-
Block-B	98	13	51	34	8	24	-	22	-	-	29	83	7	-	8	-
Block-D	154	25	87	42	15	19	5	6	-	-	60	105	42	-	5	2
Block-E & EE	150	20	84	46	21	50	2	20	-	-	41	134	6	-	10	-
Block-I	154	30	72	52	12	38	1	40	-	-	39	130	8	3	12	1
Block-K	150	22	78	50	20	26	24	30	-	-	29	129	5	1	15	-
Village Bhalasawa	150	35	90	25	7	9	2	12	41	14	60	145	5	-	-	-
Total	1006	180	534	292	92	228	37	163	41	14	276	851	73	4	75	3

wing. The total population of that area as per 1981 census was 70,301 (78.36%) of which 19,356 (21.63%) were scheduled caste (SC).

Table: 3.1(b)
Distribution of Total number of Plots Available in Each Blocks of Resettlement Colony

Blocks	*Number of Plots*
A	1890
B	1790
C	1949
D	1977
E	2897
G	2000
H	2000
I	2000
J	2000
K	2000
Total	20503

The population distribution as per sex caste and occupational status are given in Tables 3.2 and 3.3.

There were groups who were engaged in household industry. dealing in various processing and servicing as well as in repairing of machines and vehicles. 47 males and 7 females of non scheduled caste background were engaged in the above mentioned jobs. Besides, 24, SC males and 5, SC females were engaged in the same job. So far as, non-workers were concerned among the non-SC households there were 19346 males and 1459 females. And, there were 4871 SC male non-workers in the colony. (Above mentioned data are on the basis of 1991 census of Delhi). The colony comprised of people of all economic groups, ranging from very poor to rich. The various linguistic groups residing in the colony were Hindustani (a mix of Hindi and Urdu), Marathi, Bengali, Urdu, Punjabi, Tamil and Malayalam speaking.

The colony had various religious and caste groups. The majority of the people in the colony were the Hindus (85%) followed by the Muslims (10%), the Sikhs (4%). A very small number of the Christians were (0.8%) there and rest were the Jains. The various castes groups

Table: 3.2

Population Distribution of Jahangirpuri Accoding to SC, ST, Working and Literate

Type of Caste Per Profession	*Non SC ST*		*SC*		*Working Non SC*		*Working SC*		*Literate Non-SC*		*Literate SC*	
	M	*F*	*M*	*F*	*M*	*F*	*M*	*F*	*M*	*F*	*M*	*F*
Total Population	38647	31654	10499	9807	19554	1496	4927	712	20361	10240	4211	1550
Total	70301		19406		21050		5639		30601		5761	

Table: 3.3

Population Distribution of Jahangirpuri According to Agricultural and Labour Pattern

Non-SC Cultivator		*SC Cultivator*		*Non-SC Agricultural Labour*		*SC Agricultural Labour*		*Non-SC Marginal Workers*		*SC Marginal Workers*	
M	F	M	F	M	F	M	F	M	F	M	F
101	4	16	3	50	26	16	16	40	25	24	10
105		19		76		32		65		34	

residing in this area were Brahmin, Kshatriya, Kayastha, Rajput Vaishya, Nai and Kumhar. Although, the percentage of Kshatriya, Vaishya and Valmiki were relatively higher than the other caste groups. Majority of the linguistic groups were Hindustani and Punjabi speaking, followed by Bengali speaking.

Education, Transportation and Other Institution

The colony has one Industrial Training Institute (I.T.I) imparting vocational training for those who wanted to make technical career. This I.T.I. is meant for boys only. It caters both the candidates from the local resettlement and the nearby villages. Adjoining the I.T.I, there is a police station which is supposed to control the law and order situation in the colony as well in the adjoining village of Bhalasawa.

There is a hundred beded hospital runned by Delhi Government known as *Babu Jagjiven Ram Memorial Hospital.*

So far as the health care facilities of the colony is concerned, they visit to the local dispensaries.

There are eight dispensaries in ten blocks and all of these are government run and each of the dispensaries serve around one hundred fifty to two hundred individuals per day (as per the records of dispensary). 'A' block is adjoining to the G.T. Karnal Road. There were two different housing schemes which were operating within the block-'A' housing scheme, under which DDA made "Janata Flats" to sell to the public (which did not form the part of the original resettlement scheme) was not yet complete but occupied by the various immgrants perforce. Other scheme was the regular resettlement scheme.

After demolition and evacuation of the Kingsway camp hutments (1985-86) the residents were forced by the authorities to be rehabilitated in these multi-storied "Janata flats" overlooking G.T. Karnal Road. These were one room apartment with kitchen, latrine, and bathroom. These flats were given to them free of cost no rent was levied. Today the ownership is vested with these people.

Majority of the residents of this block were migrants from Kingsway Camp. A particular feature of settlement pattern was observed, i.e. those plots which were adjoining to main or motorable roads were occupied by kingsway Camps evacuees, those who had been resettled here from other places like Lucky Park, Azadpur slum or from Rana Pratap Bagh, Jhuggi, Jhopris were staying in the interior of the block. This phenomena throws light on the fact that relatively rich, resettlers came later and took the plots from original allotees at a good price, i.e. ten to fifteen thousand rupees paid extra per house. (The above fact has been confirmed by conversations) Majority of the occupants of A and B blocks were initially staying in Kingsway Camp hutments after the clearance operation of 1975-76, they were alloted trans-Yamuna resettlement colonies. But majority of them declined to go there and opted to take up plots in exchange at Jahangirpuri.

The government authorities tagged the factor of sterilisation for the residents for those plots. In conversation with a house wife, Mrs. Vimla, the things became much more crystal clear,

> ...... She told it was too difficult for them to get a plot in Jahangirpuri. They were given a plot in Nand Nagari, a trans-Yamuna. locality. She was not interested to take that so she approached to DDA office in Jhandewalan, initially they did not care but on persisting they told her that she can get Jahangirpuri if she gets sterilised...

Further she said:

> ...."They have been staying in Kingsway Camp and their place of work, children's school, ration shop and relatives as well as acquaintance have been staying in Kingsway Camp only. And Jahangirpuri is not really far off. For all practical purpose, they preferred this place than Trans-Yamuna, So, she insisted for Jahangirpuri" ...

Same thing was revealed by the neighbouring families of Mrs. Vimla,

In another conversation, Sardar Balbir Singh endorsed the statement of Mrs. Vimla in other words. On asking question about how he got two plots instead of one, he told.

> .... When he was evacuated from Kingway Camp he had a big family he could not manage in 23 square yard plot with his family, he needed more space, and only way to get more area was to get hold of more and more cases of sterilisation. So, he persuaded friends and neighbours of Kingsway Camp to undergo sterilisation and he could manage to give ten cases and he was given 46 square yard instead of 23 square yards" ....

It was clear from the above incidences that those who were

possessing more than one plot were getting at the cost self or neighbours sterilisation. To know the overall structure of the locality, it was important to know about the linguistic composition, religion and caste of the people of the area.

Linguistic Caste and Religious Groups

The linguistic groups of block A and B were comprised of Punjabi, Hindustani and minority Urdu speaking people sixty present of these people in these blocks were Punjabi speaking and 35% were Hindustani speaking and rest were Urdu speaking.

Table: 3.4 (a)

Distribution of Various Caste Groups in Block A of Jahangirpuri

Block	*Total Number of Hindu House holds*	*Brahmin*	*Kshatriya*	*Kayastha*	*Vaisya*	*SC*
A	125	9	62	3	33	18
Percent-age	100	7	43	2	34	14

It become clear from the above table that Kshtriyas were more than any other castes followed by Vaisyas. The third largest group were the scheduled castes in Block A.

The Table 3.4 (b) shows that the Hindus constitute majority and second largest groups were the Sikhs. No other religious groups were there.

Table: 3.4 (b)

Distribution of Various Religious in Block A Jahangirpuri

Block	*Total Number of Household*	*Hindu*	*Muslim*	*Sikh*
A	150	125	0	25
Percentage	100	84	0	16

Besides, knowing about the caste, religion and linguistic groups of the people it was equally important to know the family size and structure of the above two blocks. It was found that the average family size of Block A was 5.30 and that of Block B was 5.25 respectively.

The following table shows that block B is mainly composed of Scheduled casts, Vaishyas followed by Kshatriyas.

Table: 3.5 (a)

Distribution of Various Caste Groups in Block B Jahangirpuri

Block	*Total Number of Hindu House hold*	*Brahmin*	*Kshatriya*	*Kayastha*	*Vaisya*	*SC*
B	83	8	24	0	22	29
Percen-tage	100	8.5	30	0	27	34.9

So far as religious groups are concerned the Hindu were majority followed by the Sikh and the Muslims.

The Civic Amenities

Domestic (potable) water and electric supply was available for each household. But it was observed around 2% of the population in both the blocks had not taken electricity supply due to their economic constrains, although, a very few houses 0.5% did not opt for domestic tap water they managed water from hand pumps which were fitted at the end of each lane. As none of the houses had been provided with water sealed flush latrine, they had been given the community latrine which were basically connected with sanitary tank. Five pair of latrines catered each row of hundred households. However, of late individual w/c latrine been provided.

So far as the drainage system was concerned, drains were open and flanked the lanes, the lanes were kept clean by the paid sweepers of the row, "mohalla" people. There were pot holes in some of the streets that too in those streets which were in the interior of the colony. Street lamps were there but in majority of the cases it did not work because of either those were out of order or had been broken by street urchins. The defective street lights were removed after persuasion and payment of some money as bribe "Chai-Pani" to the Delhi Vidyut Board (DVB) worker.

Table: 3.5 (b)

Distribution of Various Religious Groups in Block B Jahangirpuri

Block	*Total Number Households Covered*	*Hindu*	*Muslim*	*Sikh*
B	98	83	7	8
Percentage	100	86	6	8

In 'A' Block, a market complex which was selling all sorts of domestic items. Besides, the market complex of, block 'A' had a "Super Bazar", where all the domestic consumable and non-consumable items were sold at a fixed price. And the Supper-Bazar of 'A' block caters whole of Jahangirpuri. There were two pharmacists shop which kept all common medicines, although, for the purchase of life saving drugs the colony dwellers had to go out of the colony.

In block A, there is one Delhi Public Library (DPL) which caters the heed of the area.

On enquiring about the clientele of the library from the librarian, the response was not encouraging. The librarian complained about the residents who hardly visit to borrow any book. On the contrary one young graduate of the colony, said the following words for the library.

> .... "He used to go to this library initially but gradually he stopped going and ceased to be a member, because library did not bring new books. They did not furnish readers with any information regarding other Delhi Public Library (DPL) stocks, nor did they exchange any book. Even children did not relish going there because their books were either torn or too old to be read"....

In between block A and B, there existed one community centre and adjoining to it was a higher secondary school. Although, the latter was non existent but the former was functional. The centre was meant to impart vocational training to women of the community in tailoring, sewing, music and similar domestic chores. But, the problem was of availability of teachers to teach and most of the time the teachers were on leave. According to Mrs. Raj of Block 'A'.

.... This centre should be scrapped or there should be regular monitoring of whether teachers are coming or not ....

The site meant for higher secondary school had become a place for dumping of garbage. There was an under developed play ground for children. During heavy rain, the land gets water logged and become breeding ground of mosquitoes.

The Blocks A and B are divided by the community centre and site of higher secondary school. The roads which are running between the blocks are 9 meter wide.

There was one market complex where domestic and consumer item was available. In the north west, there was a 26 meter wide road. Which is the main road of the colony and to the east also there was a relatively smaller a road.

There was one bus stop in front of block A. Besides, there is one public urinal which was on the main street facing block A. Both the blocks A and B are separated from main road by a big open drain and five under developed lawns.

THE ECONOMIC STRUCTURE OF BLOCK A & B-

Lots of similarities of different economic groups of block A and B was observed. The population of these two blocks can be divided into three major economic groups: the rich, middle and the poor respectively.

The categorisation of these groups have been done on the basic of monthly income, rich, middle income group and poor. The economic distribution of the population is given below.

Table: 3.6

Distribution of Income Groups in Block A of Jahangirpuri

Block	*Total Number Household Covered*	*Rich*	*Middle*	*Poor*
A	150	35	52	63
Percentage	100	23	35	42

Table 3.7 shows that middle and poor were relatively in same proportion numerically. Rich were the lowest percentage of people in block-A.

So far as economic groups of block-B is concerned Table 3.7 shows the three distinct groups; i.e, rich, middle and poor respectively. And, the percentage of poor people (numerically) were as high as fifty five percent.

Table: 3.7

Distribution of Various Income Groups of Block-B of Jahangirpuri

Block	*Total Number of Houses Covered*	*Rich*	*Middle*	*Poor*
B	98	13	31	54
Percentage	100	13	32	55

Various income groups can be categorised as per the type of occupations people are engaged in. Although, various sub-categories can be done but in order to maintain rationality and simplicity three broad groups were made.

The Rich Income Group:

- The rich section of these blocks were engaged in business of their own, viz. transport, running general merchandise shop, dealing in estate business.
- Doing job in government organisation.

The rich people were having two storied houses and they had built the house in such a manner that they manged four rooms. All the rich in these two blocks were having on average five members in their family and as the number of rooms were adequate they were happy about the accommodation except for the surroundings, which was mostly quite untowards for a hygienic living. All the rich people of the blocks were having their own conveyance. Besides all sorts of modern electronic gadgets of domestic usage.

The average income of these people ranged from Rs. 5000 to Rs. 10000 per month.

The Middle Income Group

Middle income groups were mostly engaged in various occupations namely.

- Working as skilled or unskilled technical hands in factories and mills in near by industrial area.
- As a government servant in public sector or in ministry
- As a owner of general merchandise shop. A group of people were dealer of day to day useable domestic items (selling those items at market places on commission basis).

The living style of middle income group was distinctly different from upper income group. They were having two to three room apartment. In cases of three rooms one room was on first floor of the house.

While conversing with one of the middle income group house wife, Mrs. Gurbinder Singh, She told

> .... They are from Kingsway Camp. Hudson Lines, her husband had a general merchandise shop in Kingsway Camp and he was still running it. They were happy there because it was a relatively neat and clean place but in Jahangirpuri they have been dumped under the Delhi clearance programme of 1975's. They were helpless had to adjust in Jahangirpuri had no other alternative, gradually they had to cope up with this situation. so, they did not mind it, her friends in Jahangirpuri were basically from Kingsway Camp. Her children were going to school in Jahangirpuri only and they also made lot of friends ....

The above case shows that even the middle income groups are not glad enough in the colony after getting evacuated from other places. So, it is a case of compromise under compulsion.

The Poor

So far as the poor income groups were concerned, their situation was very appalling. They were engaged in; daily wage labour, selling fruits and vegetables in Jahangirpuri brought from Azadpur warehouse. They worked as assistant to mason worker as "baildar" on daily wage basis.

Some of them were garbage pickers and were selling their pick at Rs. 5 per kg. Some of the women in these category were also engaged as house servants in adjoining and nearby colonies.

They were staying mostly in one room house seldom they lived in two room house. Around ten percent had television sets as they purchased it on very small initial installment with easy equal monthly instatments (EMI).

Mr. Nooruddin was interviwed to know the status of living, of the poor people of the colony. Nooruddin responded in the following words.

> .... They were staying in Lucky Park which was located in the same place. His earlier Jhuggie was double the size of the present plot. Authorities came during emergency (1975) and started bulldozing the huts and jhuggies and told that they would be given plots nearby. He had to run around for one month to get the piece of land alloted to him. The erstwhile jhuggie was spacious for his family. For the purpose of defecation all of them used to go to vast open space around the jhuggi and it was usual norm. But of late each of the latrine was stinking it was difficult to sit for a second even but they were forced to use it because they had no other choice. The children of neighbour's defecated in the gutter running in front of the door. He could not say or do anything about it ....

From the narrations of the various income groups, it became very clear that irrespective of their status they were not in a position to change or challange the system. They were compromising on all fronts as it is question of survival for them.

BLOCK C

"C" block of the resettlement colony is situated in the south west of the locality. It is flanked by open space in the left and block D on the right side. There are 1949 plots in this block. There was one market complex and primary school. In front of the colony runs a 26 meter wide road and the roads dividing the block C from the earmarked community centre and higher secondary school, besides the block C is separated from block D by a nine metre wide road.

There is a plot in between B and C which had been earmarked for higher secondary school and one plot for community centre. The area got occupied by Jhuggie and Jhopri clusters in one corner. The inhabitants of these slums were dumping their garbage in adjoining areas. They even defecated in the open area. The stray cattle, dogs and pigs roamed in the open field adjacent to those shanties.

The area became breeding ground of mosquitoes and flies as the area was full of ditches, potholes and marshy land. The area was further destroyed by the residents of block B and C as they dumped their filth in the same place.

So far, no steps was taken by the authorities to develop higher secondary school or community centre nor they were doing anything to remove those slum or improve the quality of life of the slum dwellers.

This block was highly heterogeneous in population composition, comprised of the Hindus, the Sikh, the Muslim and one percent minority comprising of the Jain, the Christian and the various linguistic groups were Hindustani, Bengali and Punjabi speaking one. One third of the houses built in this area were jhuggies on 23 square yard of plot. Eighty percent of these Jhuggies were occupied by the Bengali Muslim families of West Bengal and Bangladesh.

Caste, Religion and Family Structure

The various caste groups in these blocks were as follows:

Table: 3.8

Distribution of Various Caste Group of Block 'C' of Jahangirpuri

Block	*Total Number of Studied Hindu Household*	*Brahmin*	*Kshatriya*	*Kayastha*	*Vaisya*	*SC*
C	105	15	19	5	6	60
Percentage	100	14	18	5	6	57

The above table shows, around 57% of the Hindu population Scheduled Caste. Next as Kshatriya which comprises 18%. Brahmin 14% Kayastha 3% and 5% Vaisya respectively.

Various other religious groups who were residing in this block are as follows:

Table: 3.9

Distribution of Various Religious Groups in Block C of Jahangirpuri

Block	*Total Number Covered*	*Muslim*	*Sikh*	*Jain*	*Hindu*
C	154	42	5	2	105
Percentage	100	27.27	3.24	1.29	68

In order to study, the Muslim population in greater detail it was decided to give an extra representation of the community in block C. Moreover, the presence of Muslim in this block was more than in any other block of the colony.

The Economic Structure

The economic grouping of the population had been done in the same way as done for block A and B. The three categories were Rich, Middle and Poor respectively. The percentage distribution of the income group are given below.

Table: 3.10

Distribution of Various Income Groups in Block 'C' of Jahangirpuri

Block	*Total Number of Household Covered*	*Rich*	*Middle*	*Poor*
C	154	6	29	118
Percentage	100	4	19	77

The richer section of the community were engaged in running shops, in government service, in private organised sectors, some were in schools working as teacher. Except for self employed individuals all others were getting monthly salary. These people were earning more than seven to eight thousand rupees per month.

The middle income group were engaged in wheeling dealing of various day to day useable items and they were selling various items of daily utility, some were running tea shops, some were working in organised sector as adhoc or temporary employees. The middle income group earned on average four to five thousand rupees per month, majority were earning on daily basis either through their own enterprise or by serving others.

The poor income group formed a chunk of the population in C block. The type of jobs, the people were engaged in waste collection of garbage mainly waste paper, broken plastic objects, broken bottles and glass, dirty clothes besides, metallic waste. After collection of garbages, these were sold to "kabari" (junk) dealer.

Many poor people worked as domestic servants in various houses, worked as sweepers in the Municipal Corporation of Delhi. Some worked in bus services (DTC) and some in railway station begd for money to meet their two ends.

Almost ten percent were vendors of vegetables and fruits on the pavements.

The Social Institutions

The inhabitants of this block were mostly from Lucky Park and Mahinder Park, the above mentioned colonies were unauthorised slum located in the same place, where today stands Jahangirpuri, erstwhile colonies have been bulldozed during 1975 (as those were Jhuggies and shanties and were not authorised by Delhi Development Authorities). These people were staying in various sizes of plots (as much one could grab). They were working in near by Rajasthan Udyog area and Azadpur fruit and vegetable ware house. In block-C various caste groups who were Brahmin, Kayastha, Vaishya and scheduled castes were staying in earstwhile Lucky Park and Mahinder Park. The slum dwellers of Majnoo-Ka-Tilla too have been rehabilitated in Jahangirpuri C-block. Most of the evacuees from Majnoo-Ka-Tilla were Sansi or Khateek are of scheduled caste category. They were engaged in various odd and sundry, even some of them were excriminals engaged in various petty theft and pick pockets. Presently, they were engaged as Municipal Corporation as sweepers and many of them were posted within Jahangirpuri in various blocks as sweeper. In one conversation, the name of the head of the household of sansi family was asked. He replied as,

> ....Why his name is so important. So far as name is concerned hetells lie to the government authorities even. Though, he agreed to tell the name to the scholar, after getting convinced about his safety....

This showed that they were very seasoned criminals, over the ages they have changed to an extent to suit the present atmosphere, which is a strong factor for their very survival in todays world. It is also well known fact that, the people of Sansi and Khateek community were issued identity cards during British period in India and any inter state movement of these people used to commence with prior intimation to the nearest police station and every move by these people were thoroughly observed by the authorities. On failing to intimate in advance they used to face grave consequences.

Ex-criminals are now a days engaged in various miscellaneous jobs, from vending of tit bits to municipality sweepers. The elderly were not doing any regular service they stay at home and help in carrying out domestic chores besides looking after the grand children. It was clear from discussion that they were no more leading any gypsy life nither a life bound by the profession of killing and extortion. However, they were not shy to commit petty theft even today.

There was a large section of Bengali population living in this block. They were migrant from 24-Paraganas and Midnapur of West Bengal and a small section from Bangladesh. Eighty percent of them were the Muslim rest were the Hindu bengali. They were victim of chronic unrest and indefinite closure of jute mills in West Bengal and poor economy of Bangladesh. They have landed in Delhi as they were looking for a place which could provide them two squere of meals-daily. The scholar observed a paradox of all Muslims being labelled as Bangladeshi and the same is being used by various political parties for political milage and avoiding its duty towards its subject by using a coinage "label as Bangladeshi" so nothing need to be done.

The "Haldia Petro Chemical and Fertilizer" complex could not have come up without displacing these people. Evicted people were initially promised of one or the other job but later a very few got job in the complex and majority were evicted without adequate compensation. A few only could survive in their native place but majority went out of state, in search of livelihood. The C block migrants were mostly the retrenched workers of closed jute mills. The mills were shut down due to laxity and incapability of establishment and secondly, lesser and lesser demand of jute at national and international level led to closure of various mills.

The migration of these people was the last resort which they had to seek only when they realised that the state mills or factories were giving temporary or permanent jobs to only the party workers (the ruling left front workers) and to those who could show some or the other connection with party office or high up commrades. Moreover, at least, two or three relatives of these people were working in Delhi even before they thought of leaving West Bengal considering the pathetic condition of their friends and relatives, they (those staying in Delhi) invited them to Delhi and made them work on daily wage in the same factory where they were working.

As few of them came in search of job to Delhi. They settled in shanties of trans-Yamuna area called Seelampur. During 1975 and 1976, they were weeded out. But, in lieu they got 23 square yards in Seelampur and Jahangirpuri and majority preferred Jahangirpuri as they thought it was a better place than Seelampur to live in.

Twenty five percent of them could afford a Pukka house by taking house building loan of two thousand rupees from "State Bank of India". Although a majority could not repay the debt. And hoi-polloi made Kuccha houses and still they were staying in the same condition. For some, a Catholic Christian Missionary helped financially to build house, they written off the amount of loan for those who were living in abject proverty. Another option for these poor migrant was converstion, baptism had lot of promises for them, they had no alternative but to be baptised and immediately got house, health care and home comforts immediately.

Some seriously sick have been sent to missionary and they were treated in their own hospital called "Jivodaya" free of charges. However, a handful of the Hindu, less than one percent (0.5) after getting treated free of cost got baptised thinking of future needs both in cash and kind. Such helps were easily available for converts.

The Religious Institution

There were two small temples for the Hindu residents of the block. Although, there were no specified place for temples in this block, but people constructed temple in the empty space earmarked for woodland and park. There was only one mosque in the whole of Jahangirpuri located in 'C' block. The mosque was constructed in the DDA earmarked "Park" plot. This mosque had been mainly constructed by the Bengali Muslims. 'C' block had large number of Muslim population. The mosque authorities also organised a 'Madarasa' for the Muslim children in C block, where the Maulvi (Priest) of the mosque also teach the "Quaran". There was no gurdwara or church in 'C' block.

Housing and Habitat

There were lots of encroachments on the road side and in the open spaces, these people had come after the resettlement was built in 1976. They were mostly garbage collectors and cycle rickshaw pullers. They did almost all their domestic chores on the road side irrespective of age or sex even in some cases they were found taking bath in the open.

It was asked to one Bangali Muslim, Mr. Aslam that "why have they come to Delhi and where from. The reply was,

> ....had they not come to this place they could not have earned and lived in West Bengal, they did not find any job nor they had any land to till. A few came from Seelampur a trans-yamuna resettlement colony. Because, the colony was too much crowded and under developed, even worse than that of Jahangirpuri. They were mostly bengali Muslim, who came to their relatives in Delhi either in Seelampur or in Jahangirpuri at first and than gradually settled down in other parts of Delhi.....

The civic amenities in C block was in absolute pathetic situation, all the community latrine were stinking and non- functional. The septic tank were not cleared as per schedule, so, as and when it was opened for cleaning the residents said that they could not stay at home as the stench was unbearable.

Gutters were full of filth and, as and when it rained heavily the filth came out on the roads and in the lanes which were running in front of the houses. The street light were mostly missing or broken. Even on repeated request to fit new bulb or to change the defunct one, went to deaf ears of the authorities, because they asked for bribe which resettlers could not give as they themselves were very poor. So, nothing really moved, things remained in status-quo-ante, whether good or bad.

Hygiene and Sanitation

There was an empty space between block C and D. The empty plot was earmarked for both primary and higher secondary school. One site was meant for community centre, other for park and third one for industrial training cum work centre. But it was unfortunate to note that none of these were in existence except for one primary school, which was operating from half kuchha and half pukka house. Rest of the land was full of lot of unauthorised conglomerates of shanties. The open space was good dumping ground for the local citizens. There were myriad of burrows and dug-outs, made by man and animal giving ugly look to the whole topography. These were breeding ground for mosquitoes and the flies, after rain. These filthy things were relished by the pigs, which were later feasted on by the sweepers and other scheduled castes who were the owners of these pigs. It was realised from the study of the above mentioned blocks that the over all condition of the block C was pathetic and was further deteriorating.

BLOCK-E AND EE

Block E is divided into E and EE. It is the largest block of Jahangirpuri situated in the extreme north east of the colony. The southern side of the block is having a nine meter wide road which divides block E from Block D. The block E is centrally divided into E and EE. The total number of plots in E and EE were two thousand eight hundred and ninety seven. In front of block E runs a twenty six meter wide road (the main road) opposite to block E there is the main bus stop of the colony. In the north of EE is a nine meter wide road which is flanked by the dam cum bye pass. This was raised after the flood of 1978.

On the back side of EE, there is a "Pump house" which pumps out the drainage water from the low lying part of the colony. The pumped out drain water is siphoned into the "jheel" (a big water reservoir) which is located on the other side of the bye-pass. Most of the area surrounding block EE were marshy land full of mosquitoes and flies. Lot of filth and garbages all around was common site. There were few slums which were scattered here and there in that open space. In both E and EE, there were marketing centre and primary school. The plots which were facing the main road were mostly converted into shops selling general merchendise items to television, fan and various electrical appliances. The households which were situated inwardly (in the interior of the block) were very dingy and unclean. Because the maintenance of the lanes and gutters were not done regularly.

Regarding the status of maintenance of the lanes and drains, a lady called, Santoshi said;

> ..."They can not say anything to the sweeper of the area, as the sweepers were very adamant. The sweepers gave commission from their salary to their immediate boss and then they worked in other places, where they were paid. Even some of their well to do neighbours paid extra and got their lanes and drains clean. So, no amount of complain yielded any result. They clean their own lanes and drains personally every day....

Caste and Religion

The block comprised of all the castes and religious group, i.e. Brahmin, Kshatriya, Kayastha, Vaishya and Scheduled Caste. The various religious groups were the Muslim, the Sikh, the Christian.

Following table shows the various caste group and their distribution.

Table: 3.11
Distribution of Various Caste Groups in Block E &EE of Jahangirpuri

Block	*Total Number of Covered Hindu Household*	*Brahmin*	*Kshatriya*	*Kayastha*	*Vaisya*	*SC*
E, EE	134	21	50	2	20	41
Percentage	100	16	37	1	15	30

Kshatriya were maximum in number in this area followed by Scheduled Castes. The composition of Brahmin and Vaisya were almost in the same proportion. Kayasthas were the minority with only 1.6% of the total Hindu population. Most of the Scheduled Castes were in EE as the block was geographically most inwardly situated and the surroundings were not impressive as a result the houses were cheaper than other blocks. The distribution of the religious groups are as follows:

Table: 3.12
Distribution of Various Religious Groups in Block - E, EE of Jahangirpuri

Block	*Total Number of Covered Household*	*Hindu*	*Muslim*	*Sikh*
E, EE	150	134	6	10
Percentage	100	89	4	7

The second largest composition of religious group was of the Sikhs, consisting of seven percent of the minority group. The Muslims were four percent.

The Economic Structure

The residents of this block were categorised into three economic classes i.e., Rich, Middle and Poor respeectively.

Fifty-eight percent of the people were poor. While almost thirty five percent were middle income group. And seven percent were rich in block E. In terms of proportion of poor population, the ratio was comparable to that of the block E. In other words, both had high population of the poor.

Table: 3.13
Distribution of Various Income Groups in Block - E, EE of Jahanhirpuri

Block	*Total Number Covered*	*Rich*	*Middle*	*Poor*
E, EE	150	10	52	88
Percentage	100	7	35	58

The Rich Income Group

The rich people of this block were by and large engaged in the activities like,

- Doing salaried job in government as well in private sector.
- Running own shop of general merchandise or stationary shop.
- A small section was also engaged in transport business.

They were owner of two to three storeyed houses with five or six rooms in it, and all these were big enough and well to do house situated on the main road. Most of these rich people were non allottees. They purchased it from original allottees at a good premium. Seventy percent of the rich were Punjabi speaking population.

The Middle Income Group

The middle income group mainly comprised of mill workers, the auto rickshaw driver and were also petty shop keeper running tea stall or selling tit-bits in a temporary wooden structure (shop) on the road side.

They possessed three or sometimes four room apartment. All decorative and useful items were available in their houses. On average their family size varied from 5 to 6 members in headcount.

The poor economic section which was around sixty percent (58%) of the total population and were primarily engaged in all sorts of daily wage or temporary jobs.

They earned by pushing handcart (Thela), by working as unskilled labour in factories and mills, by working as assistant to main mason worker (baildars), and a few were engaged in cycle rickshaw pulling.

The Religious Institutions

The colony had two temples. The blocks had no earmarked plot or location for temple, but how these blocks were having temples, the curiosity was cleared up by one resident.

> .... Two temple which were there in block E were not earmarked plot for temple, those plots were meant for community latrine. If latrine were constructed there, it would have created nuisance for the adjoining houses. No one wants to live near the latrines due to stink and stench. If something else were constructed then the DDA authorities would have demolish the same for the latrine. But nobody could break the temple. So, the people decided together and constructed temple for larger benefit.

BLOCK - I

I block is situated in the south west of the main road which is dividing the blocks into two main phases i.e., I and II. It is surrounded by the group housing society on the right said, block-I is separated by 15 ft. wide road from the group housing. The houses of the group housing society was lying vacant as those were yet to be completed for the purpose of living. But, some squatters eneroached in those houses. Moreover, some of the residents of the resettlement colony were using their residential premises for commercial purpose.

And to the left of the colony, there is block-J. This block is separated from block-I, by a 15 feet wide road. On the rear side of block-I, was barren land.

I-block comprised of 2000 residential plots. Besides, it had one primary school and one market complex. The school already started functioning but the market complex was yet to start, whereas it was full of shanties. It was found that thirty percent of the houses constructed in this block were double storeyed. Half of the double storeyed houses were being used by their owner as shops in the ground floor. And they were staying on the first floor of the house. The resettlers of this block were primarily evacuees of Azad Pur, Majlish Park and Sashtri Nagar (all these colonies are located in northern part of the city).

The original land owners of these plots (fifty percent of allotees) had sold their plots, particularly the road side ones, to the highest bidders by power of attorney. Moreover, it was also observed that the road side houses were better furnished one in comparison to that of the inwardly located houses, one of the very obvious reason was that they belonged to the richer section of the people.

This block was by and large economically better of than other blocks -i.e. C, D and E. It was obvious that due to economic affluence of population the general hygiene of the colony to some extent was better than other blocks (as mentioned above). It was also noted that around five percent plots were not yet occupied and nearly two percent of the residents were staying in the thatched roof houses, although the walls of those houses were puckka.

The Poor

The poor income group were living in one room apartment, only twenty percent of the poor were staying in two room apartments.

The block had no place of worship of its own for worshiping the people of the colony had to visit to the near by blocks. In a way, the people of block-I were exception because they did not convert their plot earmarked for public latrine into a place of worship.

The Caste and Religion of the People

The caste, religion and the family composition of the inhabitants of block-I, is given below. It was found that the major caste-groups were Brahman, Kshatriya, Kayastha, Vaishya and the Scheduled Castes i.e., nai, prajapati, valmiki.

The following table shows, Vaisyas were proportionately more in number in this block. The next high proportion of the population was of the SC and the Kshatriya. The Brahmins were less in number in this area. The Kayasthas were marginally lesser than the Brahmins.

Table: 3.14

Distribution of Various Caste Groups in Block - I of Jahangirpuri

Block	*Total Number Covered Hindu Household*	*Brahmin*	*Kshatriya*	*Kayastha*	*Vaishya*	*SC*
I	130	12	38	1	40	39
Percentage	100	9	29	1	31	30

The heterogeneity of the religious groups of this block can be seen in the following table:

Table: 3.15

Distribution of Various Religious Groups in Block-I of Jahangirpuri

Block	*Total Number Covered Household*	*Hindus*	*Sikhs*	*Muslims*	*Christians*	*Jains*
I	154	129	12	8	3	1
Percentage	100	82	8	5	2	1

From the above table, it becomes very clear that majority is that of the Hindus followed by the Sikhs and the Muslims respectively. The Christians and the Jains are very small in number.

The Economic Structure

The residents of the block can be categorised into the following economic groups : The rich income group, the middle income group and the poor income group respectively.

The household wise categorisation of the families as per their income has been given below.

Table: 3.16

Distribution of Various Income Groups Covered in Block - I of Jahangirpuri

Block	*Total Number Covered Household*	*Rich*	*Middle*	*Poor*
I	154	30	72	54
Percentage	100	19	47	35

The above table shows the percentage of poor is on relatively higher side viz, almost as high as sixty. Nearly fifty percent of the population were of middle class. Around twenty percent of the people were rich in this block.

The Rich Income Group

Around fifty percent of rich people were engaged both in government sector as well as in private concern as well paid clerks and technical hands. The remaining around thirty percent were doing their business ranging from transport to cloth selling and a few were trading in general merchandise. Ten percent of the rich people were running their old shops which they were running in their previous localities. Almost the same amount of rich people were earning by renting a portion of their house.

People of rich strata posses at least three room accommodation and around five percent of people had more than three rooms. All those houses consisting of more than three rooms made on two adjacent plots of 23 square yards each. Seventy five percent of these houses were owned by Punjabi speaking business community. Rest of the people were Hindi speaking business or service class.

The middle income group comprised of sizeable number of people. They were also engaged in various types of profession, i.e. mill and factory workers, some were auto-rickshaw owner, some were driving taxis on commission basis.

Around three percent of the people were engaged in regular government service as clerks or in similar posts, some the of the people (around 5%) were working in private sectors as skilled and unskilled workers.

Nine percent of the middle income group were engaged in their own business i.e, having small grocers shop, stationary shop, small restaurant/ dhaba, some were working as agent of one or the other product on commission basis, some were also driving auto-rickshaw, and a small number of people were wheeling dealing their goods in various market places in Delhi.

Eighty percent of the people were having two room house. Around seven percent of the people in this income group were having three room house. Three percent of them were having more than three rooms (some of the houses in this category were comprised of even five rooms).

The Poor Group

The poor were in relatively more this block. Various kinds of profession the poor people were engaged in daily wage earner in most of the unorganised sectors, some were working in food and vegetable ware house of Azad Pur, some were working as labourer on daily wage basis. Some were rickshaw puller and some were running tea/tuck shops. It was also observed that mostly women and children were also working in such families. The women were working as domestic help in rich people's house within the colony or out side the colony. Some of the women were engaged in making of "papar" and some were making nuggets of various pulses (Vadi) which were sold by the agents at various outlets. A small section of these women were engaged in making handicraft items, dolls, wall hanging etc.

The children assisted their father in their profession i.e, in mason work or in carpentry. A small section of children were working as garbage collector (which are sold at Re. 1/ to Rs. 5/- per kg). Some children were selling their home made things (handicraft) in the various market places. Children were also working as low paid child labour in many of the near by factories.

BLOCK-K

'K' block is situated in the north west of the main road. It has 2000 residential plots. To the right of the block, there lies a big barren land mass, which was being used by the unauthorised squatters, for their dwellings. The same land mass was also a dumping ground of the colony dwellers. This particular piece of land was primarily meant for "Harijan Sewak Sangh". One of the influential harijan of block-K told about the background of the land in the following words.

> ...."No one was really bothered for the development of the land and most of the people are ignorant about its actual status. Even those who knew about it were not in a position to take up the matter. They are mostly busy in earning their two square of meals. Moreover. they also did not know to do anything they always looked for leadership. He could not always take up the matter as it was not possible for him to purse the matter alone. He felt that the authorities are not willing to take up the matter of their own.".....

On the rear side of the block K, there is a village called Bhalasawa. On the left of block-K, there lies Industrial Training Institute (I.T.I). In front of block-K, there is a bus stop of the Delhi Transport Corporation (D.T.C.).

Block-K had provision of two market places besides, two primary schools. Today both the schools were in operation whereas not a single shop had come up in the market complex. By and large, it was noticed that this block was inhabited by relatively richer people in comparison to that of the other blocks of Jahangirpuri.

K block had all caste groups residing there. Following table shows the various caste groups staying in K block.

Table: 3.17

Distribution of Various Caste Groups in Block K of Jahangirpuri

Block	*Total Number Covered Hindu House Hold*	*Brahmin*	*Kshatriya*	*Kayastha*	*Vaisya*	*SC*
K	129	20	26	24	30	29
Percentage	100	15	20	19	23	23

The above table clearly shows that the Vaisyas and the Scheduled Caste are numerically a good lot. Followed, by the Kshatriya and the Kayasthas, Brahmin are quite less in number.

Table: 3.18

Distribution of Various Religious groups in Block K of Jahangirpuri

Block	*Total Number of Covered Household*	*Hindu*	*Muslim*	*Sikh*	*Christian*
K	150	129	5	15	1
Percentage	100	86	3	10	0.6

The above distribution clearly shows that the Hindus are in the majority, followed by the Sikh. Three percent of them were Muslims. Whereas a small number of Christians were there. The economic composition of the people is given below:

Table: 3.19

Distribution of Various Income Groups in Block K of Jahangirpuri

Block	*Total Number Covered*	*Rich*	*Middle*	*Poor*
K	150	22	78	50
Percentage	100	15	52	33

Table 3.19 shows that poor constituted one third in K-block where as the middle class were more than fifty percent. The rich were very few in number. The rich people of this community were engaged in various types of jobs whether in private or in the government sector. Many were doing their own business, i.e. running stationary shop, grocers shop, running private schools at home, some were engaged in estate business, and a sizeable number were engaged in transport business. Those who were not doing any private or personal job they were engaged in government services, i.e. some were working as head clerk, some were skilled workers, working in mill as foreman, some were working as senior grade school teacher.

The women in this category were not doing any job to earn money. It was also observed that all the sons of the private/individual business owners go for their family business only. There was some sense of anxiety amongst those who were working in government sector because they know that their wards can not get into the same profession without taking entrance examination. Even if their children qualify any entrance examination the appointment letter can be had after greasing the palm of the babus concerned.

Like their other rich counterparts of Jahangirpuri they were also living in four room apartments, those houses with four rooms were constructed both vertically and horizontally. In other words, those who could manage two adjoining plots made their house side ways and those who could not they made vertical, double storeyed house. Around twenty percent houses were having more than six room. Below ten percent of people in this category were having less than three rooms.

The general hygiene in this area was better than the adjoining places as the rich people in this area were paying from heir own pocket for cleaning the drain which runs in front of their house. By and large, it was realised that rich were able to keep themselves clean along with their surrounding at their own expense. It was found that these rich people were staying near the main road or bus stand but not in the interior, only because they paid more for those plots.

The Middle Income Group

The middle income group were primarily engaged in self employment combined with government and private service. The types of self-employments these people were engaged in are driving auto-rickshaw on a rental basis or running ones own auto-rickshaw, one or two percent of these people were running car taxies for the tourists on rental basis. Other kinds of self employment (people engaged in) was running general merchandise shop or having a small dhaba or a tea shop. Those who were not engaged in these things they generally sold different items on commission basis to the retailers. A small fraction used to go to various market places to sell their items. In ten houses, it was noted that the women were also engaged in the earning process by means of making eatables at home and selling the same in the market, in one house it was noted that whole family was engaged in making sanitary napkins and were supplying to the standard company and earning good amount for the same.

Majority of the people were engaged as adhoc or daily wage textile mill workers in D.C.M. or Birla Mills. These people were not in a position to run their own show and did not get government jobs as well. A minority of five percent employed in government sector were working as clerks or senior grade peon. Those working in government sector were happy as they got government job, at the same time they complained of less salary which had kept them in a hand to mouth situation.

The middle strata people were also conscious of general hygiene of the surrounding, as they could not afford sweeper by payment they cleaned their surroundings of their own. But they complained about the rampage caused by stray animals in their lanes and they could not do anything as the local authorities did not cooperate with them.

The Poor

Thirty three percent of the population of this block were poor people. They belonged to different castes. They were engaged in various sorts of job i.e. doing odd and sundry and earning livelihood. They were also working in various skilled profession, like carpentry, plumbing, pottery, caning of chairs and furniture making. The above mentioned skills were getting mostly outmoded so the owner of such skills were unable to earn sufficiently. As every skill mentioned above got replaced by the mechanical substitute so their market could not sustain.

They earned more money by doing mason work, porter's job. Some were working as rickshaw puller on commission basis. A few were working in Azadpur fruit and vegetable "mandi" (warehouse) in various capacity. They purchased various fruits and vegetables and sold the same on the foot path, in kiosks, on "thelas" or they took the same in the colony and sold it there. Across the road is an industrial area known as *Rajasthan Udyog Limited.* where few of them were employed as daily wage labourers.

The women folk of the poor section were also earning to support their family. They worked as house made in near by and far away areas. These women were also working in the near by factories and mills. They were also engaged in working as baby sitters in rich people's house.

It was clear from the study that the girls of adolescence (14-16 years) were not allowed to continue the schooling in seventy percent of the cases. These girls mainly looked after the domestic chores.

These people were not in a position to have more than one room within that room they had make shift kitchen.

As block-K had no place of worship the people of this area visited other places for worshipping. So far as, *Jagaran or Katha-Prabachans* concerned those were conducted in open air at night where every caste and class were allowed to participate. The money spent for such functions were mostly collectively done, only richmen could manage such extravagenza singularly.

The colony of Jahangirpuri is flanked by the village Bhalasawa on one side. The village is the oldest entity of the area. So, it was essential to observe the impact of the resettlement on the village and vice versa. And the impact of the village on colony could be understood by studying the interaction of the two.

THE VILLAGE BHALASAWA

The village Bhalasawa is situated on the north west of G.T. Karnal Road. It spans over an area of twenty-two hectares of land. The land is mainly inhabited. In the northern side of the village, there runs a bye-pass, which is connected with outer ring road. On the other side of the bye-pass, there lies the agricultural land of the village. The bye-pass acts as dam cum road. This prevents the colony of Jahangirpuri from getting inundated (the colony got innundated during the flood of 1978). On the right flank of the village, there lies low lying open area, mostly remain water logged, also act as dumping ground of the resettlement colony dwellers. To the left to the village, there is one incomplete conglomerate of DDA flats, which is neither being completed or nor being allotted. This area acts both as garbage ground for colony dwellers and defecation spot for both the villagers and colony dwellers.

On the back side of the village, it was full of marshy land breeding ground of mosquitoes, various kinds of flies and was full of rodents and snakes.

The village had three hundred households. Seventy percent of these houses were pukka ones. Remaining twenty percent of the houses were having brick walls but thatched roofs. Ten percent of the houses were totally pukka. The village had only one proper entry facing block-K. The numbering of the houses was done very haphazardly as some of the village elderlies told the scholar that previously they did not require any number and houses were known by the head of the family or by some other identification mark or colour. The village had both water and electricity supply. Although, water connection had been taken by cent percent houses whereas less than fifty percent only had taken residential electricity connection. Street lamps were evident.

The Civic Amenities

The effuse of the village did not find any other way to get out of the village but for the open drain running centrally through the village. The lack of adequate play ground for the children of the village compensated by the open space within the two houses. The village did not have any school within its limits, so the children of this place were found visiting to Jahangirpuri schools at least for primary education.

The villagers did not have any government run dispensary on the contrary one practitioner of homeopathic medicine was visiting from outside the village every day in the evening and dispensing medicine. His dispensary was located in a residence as a result, mostly the villagers used to go to the Jahangirpuri or adjoining area for their treatment. As the village had more than ninety-five percent of Hindus and remaining Muslims, so it was obvious that they would need temple and mosque for the purpose of prayer but the village had only two Hindu temples within its precinct. The Muslims were going to Jahangirpuri to offer prayers at 'C' block mosque.

The village had a big "panchayat ghar" which was primarily built by people's contribution. It was also used by the villagers on auspicious occasions i.e. marriage, mundan (tonsure), namakaran (baptism) ceremony and for the purpose of jagaran as well.

The village was devoid of market place, so the villagers had to go to Jahangirpuri, Kingsway Camp or Kamla Nagar. As the requirement of vegetables and the grains were largely met within the village. Small items of daily requirement were also found right within the village itself.

The available amenities were not reaching up to every villager due to irregularities of some unscrupulous people who used water and electricity supply for their own illegal factories within the village. One villager said about the status of the village that with the onset of plastic industry within their village, they were getting erratic power supply. The factory owners at times needed so much of water supply leading to shortage of the water for the domestic need. So far as the employment in the local factory is concerned no one got employment there, whereas it had given employment to outsiders. And these factories were run with full consent of the authorities who were taking no punitive actions for violation of the rules as the authorities were paid on monthly basis to not to disturb in industrial activities. The pollution was so high due to the factories that the adjoining households could not keep their door or window open. Moreover, some of the houses were smudged with soot due to regular emission of factory smoke.

The village had metalled road only from Jahangirpuri to its entry point. Inside the village no metalled road could be seen.

The Schooling Process

The children below five years of age were given schooling by two private kindergardens of the locality. The well to do parents sent their children for private schooling. The craze to admit the child in that school was primarily due to its English medium training. So far as poor or middle class parents were concerned they did not send their children to school before six years of age.

It was also noted that the girls of the school age group were not going to school in eighty percent of the cases as the parents of these girls did not think it was essential to send the girl to school. Reasons for not sending the girl child has been stated as;

> .... As the boys were taking formal education so they aspired for jobs in office after completing their education, some of them in the village became teachers as well. The work load at home or field needs hardy girls. In the field the girls assisted male counterpart or fathers. Moreover, they get married early and at their in-laws place they were engaged in the same

type of work which did not demand education for the girl contrary domestic skills and physical strength was sought after....

The village had two Anganwadis (ICDS outlet at the community level to serve children), located in two different houses.

A child in the Anganwadi is taught the basic alphabets of Hindi and English. They were also taught nursery rhymes and basic numerical. During the lunch hours, these children were given daliah, (semi ground wheat) rush for collection of daliah could be seen during the lunch hours.

Various caste groups of the village

The village comprised of all caste groups i.e., Brahmin, Kshatriya, Kayastha, Vaishya, Ahir/Yadava, Jats and the Scheduled Caste. The following table shows the distribution of the caste groups.

Table: 3.20

Distribution of Various Caste Groups in the Village Bhalasawa

Village	*Total Number Covered*	*Brahmin*	*Kayastha*	*Kshatriya*	*Vaisya*	*Yadav*	*Jat*	*SC*
Bhalasawa	145	7	2	9	12	41	14	60
Percentage	100	5	1	6	8	28	9	41

The percentage profile of the caste shows domination of the Scheduled Caste, comprising of Valmiki, Nai, Prajapati and Chamar. These people were working in various capacities inside and outside the village i.e. they were working as sweepers (in the locality as well as in Jahangirpuri under Delhi Municipal Corporation), some were making shoes and selling it to retailer. Nais were doing hair cutting from house to house as they could not afford to run saloon. Many of these scheduled castes were doing odd and sundry as they were not in a position to do their traditional business due to changes in social structure of village. But, (gardner) mali were still doing gardening.

The Yadava (OBC), mainly controlled the village polity and economics. Although, they were less in number than the S.C. in absolute terms but their land holding, number of cattle, size and the number of buildings were more and well built. This community had by and large sold their land to DDA for construction of the resettlement colony. It was said that the procurement of their land had been done by the government very cheaply, so a law suit was filed against the DDA, in court of law to get further compensation. Jats were also equally rich and influential even though their number was lesser than that of the Yadava. Whereas rest of the caste groups were not dominating or powerful, they were co-existing with the others, while they were excluded from village politics.

The religious groups

The village comprised of only two religious groups i.e. the Hindu and the Muslim.

The following table shows the distribution of religious groups.

Table: 3.21

Distribution of Various Religious Groups in Village Bhalasawa

Village	*Total Number Covered*	*Hindu*	*Muslim*
Bhalasawa	150	145	5
Percentage	100	97	3

The study showed that the average family size was 5 per household. The study also showed that around sixty percent of the households were nuclear family, while the rest were joint or extended.

The Economic Structure

The village comprised of different of economic groups i.e. the rich, the middle and the poor respectively. The distribution of these groups is given in Table 3.22:

Table: 3.22

Distribution of Various Income Groups in the Village Bhalasawa

Village	*Total Number Covered*	*Rich*	*Middle*	*Poor*
Bhalasawa	150	35	90	25
Percentage	100	23	60	17

The rich of the village were mainly the Yadavas, followed by the

Jats. As these people had substantial land property since the begining their economic position never deteriorated. Moreover, their bumper production of crop with heavy yield of milk (as endowed by cattle wealth) made them economically sound. In the recent time, firstly, with the promulgation of land ceiling act followed by national emergency forced then to give away a good chunk of their land to the government. Although, the disposal was more of a compulsion rather than the free will of the villager. Procurement price of the land by D.D.A. was lower than the that of the market rate. The lump-sum money which they got by the sell of the land was used for purchasing pick up vans and in some cases trucks were also purchased.

Another way of their earning was selling of milk. Each of the Yadava and Jat house had at least two milch cows and each of the cow gave on average 12 to 13 litres of milk per day. And these families earned Rs.150/- to 200/- per day by selling milk only. Selling of milk was done only after adequate amount of milk was kept at home. Some times these villagers sold curd as well. Those Yadava or Jat who were not tilling the land nor engaged in transport business they were doing private or government service. Fifty percent of such people were in government job and rest were doing service in private organisation.

The houses of these people were quite spacious no one of the rich, middle class were having less than four rooms but for exception in four cases, it was observed that in these four cases houses comprised of eight to ten rooms.

The material possession of the rich and the middle varied in terms of number of goods but on the whole the types of possession generally did not vary. Amongst the material possession of rich, one could find the scooter or moter cycle. In twenty five households of rich family, personal cars were also found.

The poor people were the hardest hit with the changing time, as per the versions of one old timer, the poor of this area were engaged in their traditional job and as there were no technical innovation and intervention in their fields of activity, they could earn by their traditional craft and skill and feel secure too. With changing times the machine and market gave many substitution and solution to the demand of the people, now they were looking forward for new jobs. It was also clear that the modern generation had been facing great dilemma with loss of traditional occupation and at the same time by being not able to cope with new situation, they joined less paid jobs because those jobs required no special skills. Given such situation the various specific castes have taken over to sweeping and gardening in the Municipal Corporation of Delhi or in some other offices.

In the village, the poor were not allowing their women folk to do every sorts of work contrary to that of the resettlers, but those a handfal few who were working were generally working as sweepers in government organisation. Or else they helped their men folk in the field work. The material possession of these people was generally the very basic items i.e. one or two beds, six or seven bamboo cots, radio or transistor, a pair of table and chair, fifty percent of the houses had television sets acquired on hire purchase basis. Thirty percent of these people were having milching animal of their own either goat or cow or buffalo, almost the same number of households had hens and they consumed and sold eggs. The poor had pigs as their pets which were sold in market for earning besides, for the sacrifice on special ocassions.

The poor people possessed bicycle as prime mode of transportation. They did not have much land to cultivate and earn from the produce since the begining, and today the situation got grimer as most of the lands had been sold but whatever little they had were lying barren and uncultivated due to lack of money to invest on it.

Agricultural Produce of the Village

The rich people could afford to have better yield of crop. They produced sufficient crop by multiple cropping in their fields and also sold the produce in the grain market. They used tractor for ploughing, harrowing and for sowing too. They used modern fertilizers and good irrigation techniques. The seeds used by them were generally of high yielding variety (HYV). They mainly grew wheat and other vegetables i.e. cucumber, gourd, chilli, water melon in summer and occasionally maize was also sown. Besides these, cash crop like sugar cane was also grown. Although, wheat was sold but not in large quantity as production of wheat was not very heavy. Only problem faced by the farmers of this area was regular water logging of the land which turned the land into an unproductive land mass in many occasions due excessive alkilinity of the soil.

In order to assess, the life style i.e. the culture of the Jahangirpuri and Bhalasawa, one can not ignore the food habits, drinking, smoking and other addiction process which is a part of the day to day life process.

People of Jahangirpuri and Bhalasawa because of their close proximity showed a great deal of similarity in various material possessions, life style and also in seeking health care. Inspite of the similarities, it was found that some blocks in Jahangirpuri and in village Bhalasawa many behavioural variations were distinctly evident. Keeping in view the life process of these people, it was essential to discuss the variations with reference to food habits, the size and extent of problem due to alcohol consumption and drug usage.

Food Habits of the People of Jahangirpuri

The Punjabi and U.Pites and Delhiwalas had apparently similar food habits. It was essential to know whether the food habit had direct bearing on the health of the people.

Rice consumption was very rare and occasional. Rice was consumed at the most once or twice a week with "dal" or "Rajamash" (a kind of legume) that too was consumed one time either in the morning, in the lunch or in the evening. Rice was ritualistically consumed as and when someone had fever or had fallen sick as per north Indian custom.

Other preparation of rice was "Pila Chawal" or the rice cooked with fragrance, colour (turmeric) and some spices in it. *Chapati* made out of "makka" (maize) and vegetable made of mustard leaf (*Sarson Ka Saag*), relished in winter *Aloo-Panir* (Potato and Cheese), *Aloo-matar* (Potato and Pea), *Aloo-tamatar* (Potato and tomato). Sweetmeat like "Kheer", which is made of milk and rice also filled the menu of the Punjabis, Delhiwalays and UPites. One salient feature of the diet was good amount of fat consumption in the form of *ghee* or *dalda* (hydrogenated oil).

Another feature was craze for eating tit-bits from the vendors, i.e. goal gappa, chat, chole bhature. It was also observed that sometimes ladies did not bother to cook lunch they asked their children to get "chole bhature" as lunch.

The poor people were mostly hand to mouth group. They ate whatever they got. The common element of poor mans diet was Chapati made of wheat flour, with "dal" or vegetable (mostly seasonal).

It was noted that the vegetable bag of these people were stuffed with old or substandard food items as these stuffs were available cheap and were affordable.

In some cases it was observed that they managed hunger by eating tit-bits. The common practice in this group unlike that of middle and rich group was eating as and when and whatever was available at that point of time.

The Muslim and the Sikh relished non-vegetarian diet. It was observed that the Sikh did consume lot of ham, pork and chicken because mutton was costlier. Non vegetarian consumption was common among the Bengalis and among some of the Biharis. Non-vegetarian diet of these people mainly comprised of fish and cheaper goat meat. The poor of any community could manage with any type of non vegiterian stuff they did not show any hesitation to take non-vegetarian diet like beef or poor quality pork. Restriction of non-vegetarian diet was noted amongst the Brahmins and the Ahirs.

Milk, Tea and Its Consumption Pattern

Although, the topic may look very mundane and irrelevant, but the affordalitity of milk on regular basis to every one was really difficult and so the consumption pattern changed from one section of the people to other.

The middle income group could not afford milk regularly, as a result, it was also observed that most of the children in this group took tea rather than milk. Milk consumption for the poor was a distant dream, in ninety percent of the houses, the remaining could afford to take only hundred or hundred fifty grams of milk per day. The distribution of milk within the family was also erratic viz, a small child below six years of age or an earning hand or the head of the family were the lucky few who could get more to drink. One can find a clear cut distinction in the milk consumption pattern from rich to poor.

On the issue like, whether the child at home takes milk every day or not, it was found that, it is luxury for many houses to have milk every day. One of the ladies during conversation on milk consumption said :

> .... Milk is fifteen rupees a litre and her husband earns four thousand rupees a month and they are six members. Somehow, she manages half a litre a day and that is how all the four children get tea to drink. And now they do not want milk, they ask for tea only. So, far as the adult members of the family is concerned the husband and herself never think of taking milk.

On the whole, it was realised that the consumption of tea initially starts as substitute of milk but after some time it becomes more of an addiction than merely addition to milk. The concept of breakfast or snacks vary as per the economic status of the family, rich and middle class generally take bread as snack. The poor generally take left over *chapati* (bread) of the previous night along with tea as break fast.

It was also noted amongst these people consumption of milk was not so common. The biharis and the bengalis prefered more tea than milk even if they could afford milk. By and large, the food habits amongst the middle strata and the rich did not vary much except the quality of food items being consumed. It was noted that the rich did not bother purchasing things at the quoted price of the hawker and no bargaining is done, on the contrary demand for better quality items were made, whereas the middle class did bargain and also did not want to compromise with the quality. In the process, they were mostly the losser.

It was observed by the scholar that the cooking media amongst the well to do was hydrogenated oil or Dalda. Less than five percent of the rich were able to use pure ghee. Moreover, it was reported that the children in the family did not relish ghee. A little deviation was observed in case of middle class family, they were generally taking refined, palm oil. Only one or two percent were taking hydrogenated oil. Consumption of milk was certainly less in the middle class in comparison to the richer section.

In contrary to such food habits the poor were not in a position to take vegetables or ghee from the hawkers or from the local shops rather they purchesed from *mandi* (warehouse) which is located very near to their colony. They purchased vegetables which were sub-standard. The price of such items were also less.

The economic constraints made this people eat any thing, whatever they could afford to take, in this process they mostly made themselves sick on many accounts. Moreover, the water they drank although potable but not kept properly, as the bucket full of water sometimes kept out in open and were contaminated by cows, birds and some times by the dogs, as a passer by thirsty animal quenched its thirst there.

Food Habits of the People of Bhalasawa

The food habits of villagers is related mostly to their agricultural pattern. They consumed their own agricultural produce. Instead of purchasing from the open market.

The food habits of these people were more tradition bound. In other words, the villager's staple diet was wheat *chapati* and various vegetables which were grown in their fields. It was also observed that the most coveted dish for these people was *chapati* made out of maize flour and preparation of mustard (which grow in abundance during the winter seasons). This is enjoyed by one and all, irrespective of caste, creed or religion. Particularly, in winter in every house this particular preparation was evident. Consumption of milk amongst the richer section was as high as 250 gm. to 500 gm. per day per person. Besides, milk the people of this category were taking various other derivatives of milk, i.e. curd, butter milk, butter, skimmed milk and other milk preparation. It was also noted that these people had a tendency to take most of the vegetables raw from the field viz. carrot, radish, spinach and sugar cane etc. such type of eating habit was not only restricted amongst the rich, the poor also enjoyed such raw eating. Such type of consumption was not only time saving but also highly nutritive. However, this eating behaviour also made GI patients as in some cases the germs enter live in the body as it is not baked or cooked or properly cleansed and caused gastro-intestinal problems.

Drinking, Smoking and Other Addiction Pattern

The poor were consuming good amount of country liquor which was readily available in an around the locality. It was locally known as "gattoo". Most of the heavy vehicle drivers as well as lathe machine workers were the main consumer of local brew. Most of these people consumed less solid diet, like *chapati*, vegetable, *dal* but they were addict of gattoo. Any kind of drink was most welcome as status symbol and a means of marry making for the inhabitants of Jahangirpuri.

Drinking was quite common amongst the lower economic group of people. Drinking was not confound to a particular caste or religious group. One of the resident said that;

> ... he drinks casually when he gets totally exhausted. And his profession is too much demanding. When he drinks he gets relaxed and drink also act as booster to work more and more. But, he does not eat non-vegetarian food.

On enquiring that does he think driking is better than taking non vegetarian food. He said,

> ... Drinking increases friendship. Act as booster and it also gives status, on the contrary eating meat means committing sin so he never takes non-vegetarian diet....

It was found that such believes were well embedded among majority of the people of the colony.

Consumption of liquor has different connotation for different economic group or in other words, rich attributed different meaning to drinking than the poor. Drinking is more of a status symbol amongst the rich and the middle class people. Moreover, the business men of the community finds drink handy to get their business deal materialise in a drinking session. Whereas, in case of the poor section it was noted that they often consumed it only after they had been treated free by friends or relatives.

Smoking of tobacco was as high as seventy-five percent. It was observed that smoking was very much sex bound as only less than one percent of women were addict. The average age of starting of tobacco smoking was fourteen to fifteen years. Many boys going to higher secondary classes were smokers. As the school going children found it difficult to purchase individually every day, so sharing and pooling of money for the cigarettes or smoking of bidis was very common. It was also noted that there was always a kind of negligence or deliberate ignorance amongst the teachers, as they at the first instance overlooked and did not check the habit and it was only checked when these boys were regular smokers. They said that the parents must look into it, they shouldn't give pocket money to their children. Moreover, these boys did not smoke in front of the teachers at all so, teachers expressed helplessness to control them.

Seventy percent of the people smoked cigarette or bidi irrespective of caste, class or religion. Smoking was relatively less among the women, but it was noted that the women of lower caste did smoke. Alcohol consumption was less amongst the Muslims. Chewing of pan was common (cent percent) amongst the men and women folk of the Muslim community.

Drug Trafficking

Drug trafficiking was pronounced amongst all the economic strata of the people but paradoxically enough it was more common amongst the poorer section of the society. The drugs were imported from outside the colony but found a good ground amongst the unemployed, the auto-rickshaw drivers, the retrenched employees and also amongst few pleasure seekers (new addict enjoying the kick of it).

The community of drug takers unite together mostly in the evening in one or the other corner of the colony and share the drug together. As the expenditure was too high so it became essential for them to share. Addiction was not contingent upon age caste or class, but no women addict were seen.

Through an exhaustive conversation with the colony members it was found that no one of the parents or family members liked that their household member should be called addict. The colony members were annoyed with the activities of the addicts as they even stole and sold others goods and purchased drug out of it. On the whole, it was found that the peopie of resettlement were not at all in favour of addicts or drug peddlers. This kind of situation was thriving on the basis of local illegitimate support of the law and order authorities combined with the external forces, i.e., by the help of local politicians and the rich addicts who did not belong to this place but found it a heaven to deal and peddle in drug. The following case study revealed the problem of drug problem of the area.

A house wife Mrs. Kanta narrated an episode. As she was asked does any one of her family member drink, she told:

> .... Her husband was a handsome personality but as he got retrenched from the regular job, he was non-plussed by worries and anxieties, he was pulling a cycle rickshaw and was earning for the family during post retrenchment period, but to overcome various stresses, he started to consume hooch, sold in the colony by various hawkers, locally known as "gattoo". He would consume it every night (inspite of breathing trouble and weak health) and gradually he became addict....

It was found that the police do not take strong action against gatto sellers.

On detailed queries and conversation with the local residents and the enforcement authorities in detail. It was realised that;

The bootleggers bring the hooch from out side the colony and they sell it in a disguised manner. The local brew mostly act as element of enticement for those who employ the able bodied unemployed adult male for their shops or local factories. It was given to the hoodlums by the local political goons to get the party work done. In other words before and after any election of either local bodies or national level the illicit liquor is must for all the local workers. Given such background flow of drinks in the colony remain unabated.

Farida, a Bengali Muslim girl around eighteen years of age, told about the drug trafficking in block-C in particular, regarding smoking habit in her family, she said:

> .... Her brother a twenty years old, boy being unemployed vagabond, although 6th pass having no job. He hardly cared for home he used to arive late night, stoned, father and mother got fed up with him. For few days, he was in police custody, as the father went to police station to set him free but they told him to give thousand rupees to release him, the father a poor "thelewala", what could he do but for selling his thela and his wrist watch to pay thousand rupees to the police and then the son was released. But, as soon as the son came home within no time again he started taking smack. Parents tried to make him understand in many ways that drug is bad for health. Parents also told him that it is against the shariya of "Quaran", but he did not care and still continues to take drug...

A gang of three was busted by police, they were all non-residents of Jahangirpuri who were peddling smack in the colony. A scooter taxi driver who was a resident of the colony was taking drug and also became a drug conduit for the colony youngsters. The scooter driver was hardly going out with his taxi because he was making commission on the smack deal in the colony. It was also unfortunate that the target of drug, in the colony were mostly unemployed, illiterate Bengali Muslim youngsters, they were selling their household goods for the drug. Even some of them were pilfering other's goods as well....

Farida, was asked "What does the patrol police do, she replied,

> ....patrol police does not catch the drug takers because they are given some amount of cash (bribe) to overlook, all the nuisance...

The above incidence indicates that drug has made in road into the colony irrespective of religion or income group. The above description demands a close look into the existing law and order and political scenario which was larglely responsible for such misdemanours.

Duration of Working Hours

As it had been mentioned earlier regarding the type of occupation of the people which ranges from rickshaw pulling to clerical job as well as petty shopkeeping. Those who were not serving at any place they had their own business i.e., tea shop, fruit and vegetable shop, gorcers shop or working as market place vendors of various items.

In order to find out that on average how many people were working, how many hours in a day, the scholar asked regarding their working hours in a day.

Table 3.23 shows that among the poorer section-seven percent of the people were working from three to six hours only. Sixty-three percent of the poor were working six to nine hours a day. In other words, seventy percent of the total poor were working for optimum duration to earn their livelihood. Twenty-one percent of the poor were working for more than nine hours a day (which includes over time). And only eight percent worked even more than twelve hours a day. Those who were working more than twelve hours a day were running their own show and in order to earn more they were sitting for longer duration.

Table: 3.23
Distribution of Working Hours Per Day Per Individual in Different Income Group

Income Group	*3 to 6 hrs.*	*6 to 9 hrs.*	*9 to 12 hrs.*	*12 hrs. and more*
Poor	7	60	20	8
	(7.36)	(63.15)	(21.0)	(8.42)
Middle	8	95	58	5
	(4.81)	(57.22)	(34.93)	(3.01)
Rich	14	30	10	-
	(25.92)	(55.5)	(18.51)	(0)
Total	29/315	185/315	88/315	13/315

So far as middle income group was concerned, around five percent were working three to six hours a day. Fifty seven percent were working six to nine hours a day. Around thirty five percent were working nine to twelve hours a day. Out of these thirty five percent, ninety percent were earning overtime for the extra hours of work they did. Only three percent were working more than twelve hours a day. All of them were self employed so they sat and relaxed as long as they wanted.

It was also noted that amongst the richer section, around twenty six percent of the people were working three to six hours a day, in other words they were engaged in various types of self endeavour, rich were doing job in various private and government concerns. It was found that nearly eighteen percent of the rich were doing their own business and they were sitting from nine hours to twelve hours a day to earn more.

The above table shows that nearly fifty nine percent of the workers of the colony and the village were doing six to nine hours a day duty in order to earn their bread and butter. And around twenty nine percent were working more than nine hours and some of them were even working for twelve hours a day. And a very small four percent were engaged in excessive amount of work, 12 hours per day.

Political Awareness and Affiliation of the People

The study showed very clearly that the people of this area were voter of the ruling Congress party. Although, they admitted openly that ruling party was using them as vote bank but in turn were not giving anything. But the only explanation given for such behaviour was, "every one is thief, so, why not to elect known one." It was also admitted by them that the only good thing the ruling party have done that they have regularised the slums within the resettlement.

Such regularisation and legitimisation defeated the very concept of the resettlement. So far as the village was concerned, the residents of the area invited the member of parliament and who showed overwhelming concern to improve the living condition of the area, but inspite of the assurances nothing significant was done for the betterment of the area. Only all sorts of assurances had been given during different elections but in vain, as things remained status quoante.

So far as the of names of the metropolitan councillor and municipal councillor, member of parliament were concerned people knew their name address and telephone number. But it was clear that these public figures did not brother until or unless some group applied pressure on them. It was a common belief that the only way by which they could get the work done is to give cash (which is taken for so called "party fund").

So far as local level political maneuvers were concerned, it was realised that the regional politicians would pick up some local goons, who were given some training how to protect and promote the party interest and in turn these goons were given some fringe benefits i.e. job or a small dealership, cash was also given on successful completion of the work, allotment of best plot in the locality to the party workers and in case of repeated success in achieving the target or entrusted mission, party ticket was also offered to these stooges. The power structure was designed and determined by the power elites who controled the politics of urban life of Delhi. It was more obvious in case of the politics of resetlements, where the low browed politicians were tampering with the faith of these under dogs. These resettlers were used as vote banks to maneuver their power politics. Because of this type of polity, it was found that all the three economic groups were helpless in improving their condition of life, it could only be improved if the power brokers desired so.

Culture Change: A Brief

The life process of the resettlers and the villagers were confound to three economic groups poor, middle and rich respectively. The life of the poor was a picture of extreme low form of human existence, assessed through a detailed account of day to day life cycle replete with misery, deprivation, exploitation unemployment and under-employment. This provided one subsculture and the life style of the rich provided other extreme in the total culture of the resettlement. The life of middle class was at the intermediary state. A continuum between two extremes of the life process of the resettlement, the rural life style on one hand and the urban on the other was visible in the composite culture of Jahangirpuri. In other words, resettlement looked like a phoenix of slum.

However, the culture of the resettlers and the villagers changed materially but at a price they paid in lieu was exorbitant and in the process severed their connection from their originality. The culture of the people changed on many accounts beyond recognition and an unhealthy trends have set in. A trend which nither gave any real benifit to the resettlers nor did it envisage anything good or substantive for the future of the resettlement in particular and for the city of Delhi in general.

A change which ensured nemesis of original culture of the resettled having a tremendous impact on the sub-cultural entities, i.e., economy, health, polity and socio-cultural practices due to the vagaries of resettlements life style. It also dislodged those communities from their base in gradual manner. The dismemberment of the cultural root combined with ensured nemesis of resettlers culture projects a gloomy future of these people. These communities not only loose their identity but also potentiates a snow ball effect of gradual decadence of the city life and also engendered an urban society which unmindful and non responsive to such a painful degeneration.

4

HEALTH CARE FACILITIES OF JAHANGIRPURI AND BHALASAWA

Local Health Care Infrastructure

It is an imperative to know about the available health care infrastructure within and outside the resettlement colony and the village. The composition of the health care facilities are so heterogeneous that each deserves an independent assessment in order to have greater comprehension of overall health care practice of both the resettlers and the villagers.

To cater the health care need of the colony, Municipal Corporation of Delhi (MCD) and Delhi Administration have made some provisions of dispensaries and polyclinics. Besides, every block has nearly fifteen to twenty private practitioners. As a general practitioners starts his clinic on one hand at the same time at least one or two practitioner close down his clinic due to non profitable market. Intermittent opening and closure of clinics made it difficult to ascertain the exact number of private health care outlets.

The dispensaries of MCD and Delhi Administration have a particular staff structure and working pattern. Before anything else is discussed it is better to give the structure of the various dispensaries in detail which would reflect the existing health care structure of the colony.

Block-A : Health Care Amenities

"A", block Maternal and Child Health (MCH) unit has two lady doctors, two Auxiliary Nurse Midwives (A.N.M), One trained midwife, four lady health visitors, one peon cum chowkidar and one sweeper. This dispensary is run by Municipal Corporation (MCD).

The dispensary is officially open from 9 A.M. in the morning to 3 P.M.. in the evening, although, the doctors are available upto 1 P.M. and thereafter the doctors are not found in the dispensary. This dispensary is supposed to cater the needs of block A, B, C and H, and some adjoining areas other than the Jahangirpuri, it caters Mahinder Park and Bhadola village (near Adarsh Nagar).

In this dispensary, the ante and post natal check-ups were done for the mothers. Besides, the children of pre-school groups were also looked after. The check-up under the national health programme regarding M.C.H. CSSM is also carried out, the programme essentially takes care of,

1. Vit-A Iron and follic acid prophylaxis for expecting mothers.
2. For the new born Immunisation programme of D.P.T., Polio, Tetanus, measles and T. B.
3. They are also supposed to carry out the verticle health programme dealing with mother and child, as well as Pulse Polio Immunigation (PPI) programme.
4. Also to administer Hep-B vaccine for new born although restricted in some areas of the city.

Besides, these programmes family planning activities were also looked after by the block "A" dispensary. Both types of contraceptives were available, condoms for male, copper-T and oral pills for females were also to be disbursed.

A-block has one Employee State Insurance (E.S.I.) Dispensary this is primarily meant for the people who are working in mills and factories.

The block "A" dispensary of E.S.I. had six doctors of whom two were lady doctors, five pharmacists, five ANMS, two dressers, one *aya* and four peons along with three sweepers. It had one head clerk cum U.D.C. one cashier and three lower division clerks.

The working hours of this dispensary is 7.30 A.M. to 1.30 P.M. and 1.30 P.M. to 7.30. P.M. It runs in two shift basis. The E.S.I. dispensary caters nearly seven hundred patients per day. And, it has nearly 15000 card holders who can come and have treatment and medicine from this dispensary.

Like "A" block M.C.D. dispensary for M.C.H. this dispensary also does not have facilities for delivery. But inception of copper-T was taken care of in E.S.I. dispensary.

Both the M.C.D. and E.S.I. dispensaries remain close on Sunday, and on national holidays. The malaria workers were not available in these dispensaries.

Block-B Health Care Amenities

The B Block dispensary is run by Delhi Administration, the staff structure of the dispensary is as follows: two doctors, one pharmacists, one ANM, one dresser, one nursing orderly and three sweepers cum chowkidars. In the morning hours (8AM-1PM), the allopathic treatment and medicine was given while in the evening shift the same dispensary provided Homeopathic facilities for the patients of the colony. The latter starts from 2 P.M. to 8 PM. every day, except for the Sunday.

The B-Block dispensary was the oldest general dispensary of the colony. The family planning advices and facilities too were available, contraceptives could be had from the same dispensary. The need to open 'C' and 'H' block Delhi Administration dispensaries were felt only when the rush at 'B' block became unmanageable.

The medical officer of 'B' block said that as per general rule for every two hundred and fifty patients per day there will be two doctors and on exceeding that limit it will have one more doctor and the dispensary with three doctors and other para-medicos will be called, "up-graded dispensary". But, it was realised that by having an upgraded dispensary it will not serve the purpose, so there came the polyclinic in C-block and the H block dispensary respectively. Although, both came up after 1978 flood of the Delhi (Jahangirpuri was one of the worst affected colony during the flood).

The 'B' block dispensary not only gives medicine to its own patients but also to that of block C. This dispensary has malaria personnel in the pay role of MCD, whose, attendance is also maintained in the 'B' block dispensary. The blood testing for malaria is done by the staff of block "B", although his local head office is situated at J-Block M.C.D. dispensary which is basically an Ayurvedic dispensary. The medicine prescribed at 'C' block polyclinic is also given at the same polyclinic, the same medicine can be had from 'B' block dispensary as well.

The C Block Polyclinic

The 'C' block, Delhi Administration polyclinic is a type of upgraded dispensary. This dispensary has three doctors, one of general medicine, one lady specialist, one child specialist one ANM, one staff nurse, one nursing orderly and one sweeper cum chowkidar. But it is unfortunate that since its inception it did not have any child specialist till date. This polyclinic has also a provision of one opthalmologist coming from A.I.I.M.S. on two alternate Mondays of the month.

This polyclinic has only single shift facility. The 'C' block dispensary has facilities for inception of contraceptives and malaria detection.

D-Block Dispensary

D block has M.C.D. run Maternal and Child Health (M.C.H.) centre. The structure of the dispensary is given below, two lady doctors, four A.N.M.'s one trained midwife, three lady health visitors, one peon and one sweeper. The activities of the dispensary is almost same as that of 'A' block M.C.H. dispensary. These dispensaries do not have beds for delivery, so the A.N.M. or trained midwife goes to the expecting mothers house to carry out delivery. The paramedicos of 'D' block take the sterilisation cases to Babu Jagjivan Ram Memorial Hospital or Kasturba Gandhi Hospital. If the case is of male child she gets Rs. 501/- and it is of female she gets Rs. 301/-. And for the insertion of Copper-T, Rs. 50/- is given to the lady (client) by the government.

But, it was also said that if the copper-T got inserted by some other authorities other than the A and D block M.C.H dispensary, no responsibilities are taken by them in case of any mishap due to IUD complications. If the lady goes to the dispensary of A or D for removal of the IUD, there the staff does not take any responsibility for post removal complication as well. The D block dispensary covers the cases of E, E E, G, I, J besides, village Bhalasawa.

E-Block Health Care Unit

The E block dispensary is run by a Christian Missionary called "Sisters of the Destitute". The dispensary came into existence in 1978 immediately after the havoc of the flood. Although, the dispensary is nearly defunct today.

This dispensary has locally appointed doctor who is paid monthly for the duty he renders from 9.30 A.M. to 12 P.M. It has three locally appointed nurses who are paid Rs. 4500/- month, who renders duty for the two different shifts 8.30 A.M. to 1 P.M. and 2 P.M. to 7 P.M. respectively. Thirty seven locally appointed Community Health Workers (CHW) (of whom only one was Christian) worked for four hours a day and were paid Rs.1500/- per month. There were two T.B. workers for whole of the colony and the C.H.W.s were covering E, EE. D,C, and Juggis for C block. The Community Health Workers were generally engaged in M.C.H. activities and family welfare motivation campaign. There was one Chowkidar and one lab technician for confirmation of T.B. cases.

Primarily, this dispensary had two levels of liaison activities:

1. It is an off-shoot of the same missionary hospital which is working in a large scale at Ashok Vihar (a colony situated nearly 4 km away) known as "Jivodays". A sound referral system to Jivodaya hospital was available for the patient, who visited for one or the other treatment at E-Block dispensary.
2. The Kingsway Camp R.B.T.B. hospital also has referral with Jivodaya. The cases of T.B. were detected by sputum test in the local dispensary and for X-ray patients were referred to the hospital or if the case had been treated for some time at R.B.T.B. and the patient belongs to Jahangirpuri then free of cost medicine was given from this dispensary to such patient, as the medicines for the detected cases was given to this dispensary by R.B.T.B. hospital.

But in case when the patient came of his own for treatment and is not a R.B.T.B referred one, then money was charged for medication to non referred patient.

This dispensary had five beds for delivery cases, delivery of a child was not done free of cost. It had one malaria detection technician. And at times experts from Jivodaya did come for giving consultancy service. Money was charged from every patient depending upon the status of the patient. From an extremely poor patient only one rupee was charged for treatment and two to three days medicine was also given. Similarly, one may be charged Rs. 5/- or Rs 10/- or Rs. 20/- as per the patient's economic capability. This missionary dispensary also actively participated for family welfare and sterilisation campaign as and when they got directive from the government.

Dispensaries of Block H and J

The dispensary in 'H' block is a general dispensary and is run by Delhi Administration. The resettlers from other blocks also avail services here. The staff structure of the dispensary is as follows, it had two doctors, three pharmacists, one ANM, one lab assistant, one dresser, one nursing orderly and three sweepers cum chowkidars. This dispensary came up later to share the load of block B. This dispensary gives its own medicine unlike that of C block. It has got one M.C.D. malaria worker attached to it.

There is one M.C.D. run Ayurvedic dispensary in block-J. This dispensary functions from 8 A.M. to 3 P.M. every day except on Saturday. Usually, M.C.D. and Delhi Administration run dispensaries work half a day on Saturday, Sunday the dispensaries remain close. The staff pattern of 'J' block dispensary is as follows, one medical officer, two pharmacists and one peon. This dispensary catered four hundred to four hundred fifty (which comprised of both old and new cases) patient a day. It had direct link with one Ayurvedic hospital which is two and a half kms away, known as *Haiderpuri Ayurvedic Hospital* which had eighty beds and an X-ray unit along with it.

In cases of complication, the patients were also referred to the Ayurvedic hospital.

The J block dispensary mainly catered the patients who were not satisfied with the Allopathic treatment, (as claimed by the dispensary doctors). They mainly treated G.I.T. disorder, Leucorrhoea and worm infested children. But the cure rate of chronic Leucorrhea cases were high in Ayurvedic system as per the claim of the doctors of the dispensary. This Ayurvedic dispensary caterd whole of Jahangirpuri and the Bhalasawa village. Besides, the Ayurvedic dispensary this building accommodated all the M.C.D. malaria staffs. The DDT spraying staffs were also stationed there. The DDT storage was also done in the same building. Even those corporation staff who sprayed pesticides in the gutters and water in the ditches report first at J block dispensary before going to duty. The salary of the malaria staffs was disbursed in the same dispensary. Testing of malaria slide were being done in the same building.

However, the Babu Jagjivan Ram Memorial Hospital has all the provision for malaria testing.

Babu Jagjivan Ram Memorial Hospital

This is one of the two resettlement colony hospitals, i.e. Madipur and Jahangirpur. This hospital became an entity almost after eighteen years of colonies existance. This is a hundred beded general hospital (the first one was built in Madipur resettlement colony). This hospital is manned by fifty specialists. This hospital has three wards and all the routine health care facilities, i.e. medicine, surgery, paediatrics, gynae and obstetrics, Orthopaedics, E.N.T, ophthalmology skin and other non-clinical essential supporting facilities. It has dental specialists too. This hospital has also provision to treat the mental health problem cases. The facility is provided twice a week by Institute of Human Behaviour and Allied Sciences of Delhi. The complicated cases are referred to various other hospitals of the city. However, the OPD caters 1700-2000 patients of different ailments daily. This hospital not only caters Jahangirpuri it also caters the patients of adjoining area. Unfortunately, the rush in the hospital forces duplication or triplication of patients in one bed. This hospital also provides ambulatory services for the colony and adjoining area. It was unfortunate to know from the discussion with the local residents that the emergency cases were not admitted at night, contrary they are referred to Hindu Rao or St. Stephens Hospital. The authorities said that they are handicap due to lack of doctor and staffs at night combined with short supply of medicines and lack of essential equipments of care.

The Local Private Clinics

Besides, the above mentioned government facilities there are many private clinics available throughout the colony. There are at least fifteen to twenty private practitioners practising in each and every block. They range from Licentiate Medical Practitioner, (there was one LMP at C block, who was a Bengali Muslim had come from Bangladesh), Registered Medical Practitioner, B.I.M.S. and M.B.B.S. Besides, there were some homeopaths and nurses and compounder turned doctor.

The fees ranged from Rs. 20/- to Rs. 150/- per patient. Higher charges were paid to the M.B.B.S. doctors. Some of the M.B.B.S practitioners happened to be ex-medical officer of Hindu Rao or Safdarjung hospital. As a result at times, they referred the patients to their fellow doctor colleagues in those hospital and enjoyed kudos from patients.

The Anganwadis of the Colony and the Village

This area had hundred and nine Anganwadis, which were managed by Bhalasawa community development block ICDS schemes. The Anganwadis could be found in all the blocks and in the village of Bhalasawa as well. These Anganwadis are supposed to cater the children of pre-school age group. Each Anganwadi had one Anganwadi worker and one assistant, both were female staffs. The child is enrolled by the Anganwadi as soon as he becomes a toddler. The mid day meal is supposed to be given to these children besides, teaching the alphabets Hindi and English both and arthematic through games.

One of the major activities of the Anganwadi was to make cards for the children which in turn taken by the child's parents to the MCH care unit for immunisation; viz, vaccine of DPT, B.C.G. Polio, measels, etc.

Various malpractices and pilferages in these Anganwadis have been reported by the local residents. And, it was also noted that relatively richer people of the colony had strong apathy for the institution and its activities and many simply thought it is below their dignity to send the children to Anganwadis because according to them it is meant to cater the poor and needy only. Anganwadis were supposed to carry out the I.C.D.S. programmes, as well as help implement all other health programmes (mainly immunisation).

The patients of the resettlement colony and the village were free to approach any hospital or private nursing home for their treatment. It was found that the patients after getting disappointed from local government and private health care facilities, majority approached to Babu Jagjivan Ram Memorial Hospital and for female and children to Kasturba Gandhi and Kalawati Saran as well. And those who could afford visited St. Stephens for their treatment.

Local bone setters were also frequented by the resettlers and villagers. And in many cases the spiritual healers are also sought after and were reliable practitioners for many of the sufferers. It was observed that in those cases the element of faith and belief was quite stronger than objectivism or rationality. Spiritual healers were the ultimate solution for chronic and long ailing patients.

The government and the private health care institutions of the resettlement colony are important organ of health culture for both the resettlers and the villagers. It is equally important to know about these organisations as because these are one of the key component of referral system for major hospitals which happened to be the key player in the maintanance and up keep of people's health in the modern context.

Understanding of the hospital and its infrastructure is very essential as no health care concept or model of contemporary treatment system is complete without it. Similarly, the treatment process of the Jahangirpuri resettlers and the people of Bhalasawa starts initially form the local dispensaries (in majority of the cases) and finally lands up in hospitals like, Babu Jagjivan Ram, Hindu Rao, Kasturba or St. Stephens in most of the cases. Majority goes to Babu Jagjivan Ram as it located within the colony for their treatment, failing which, medical shopping starts vehemently.

It was also felt during conversation with the local residents that the available and affordable health care institutes and facilities were primarily a necessary evil for interaction, in cases of physical and mental indisposition visit to dispensary or hospital is not a welcome proposition in the system of health care practice of the resettlers or the villagers in a natural course. It is also essential to understand the microsituation vis-a-vis the social and cultural set up. The microsituation is typified by confrontation between clientele and hospital as institutions, a situation that work more at cross purpose rather than identifying itself close with the culture and values of the people and the community. Microsituations involving patients and hospital staff, and their social interactions in terms of role expectations and unofficial behaviour, are analysed from the perspective of symbolic interactionism and the definition of the situation. The microsituations include reference to: illness definitions; concepts of the hospital; diet and its complications: ritual and secular status in the ward; pollution; blood as limited resource; attendant in the ward; the patient or sick role; and instrumental *vs.* expressive aspects of the nursing role in relation to the social structure of the clientele. There is a need to develop an institutional health care which will delineate, represent and predict a client-institutions interaction in societies where the social structure of secondary institutions varies with that of primary groups and institutions.

5

HEALTH CULTURE OF THE COMMUNITY

It is necessary to take a holistic view of all the cultural parameters which relates health and health services of a community with overall culture, while carrying out various anthropological as well as behavioural studies in the field of health a holistic perspective gives a clear and comprehensive insight of the situation. For developing such a holistic view, it is necessary to consider simultaneously the various cultural factors which generate certain health problems in a community, the cultural perception and the culture, meaning of various health problems encountered by the community and the various institution that the community either as a diffusion of an innovation from outside or as an intrinsic innovation by the community. It may be observed that all these aspects related to health problems and health practices can be studied only in the context of overall culture of the community. This composite of (a) cultural perception and cultural meaning of health problems (b) the various cultural devices that are available and accessible to members of a community for dealing with health problems and (c) the consequent behaviour of the community in response to these health problems which is generated as a result of interaction of culture perceptions and cultural meaning of health problems and the cultural devices for dealing with them has been defined by Banerji,[1] as "health culture". In this context, establishment of a network of health services by the government and other agencies (e.g. missionaries) represents a purposive intervention to bring about changes in the health culture not only by making available and accessible medical institutions to populations, but also by actively promoting the use of some aspects of the services

1. Banerji D., *Poverty Class and Health Culture*, Prachi Publication, 1982.

(e.g. family planning, vaccination, D.D.T spray etc.) within the populations. Health culture therefore becomes an integral component of the overall culture of a community. The culture of a community also directly influences its health culture because certain cultural practices such as child rearing, food and drinking habits, pregnancy and child birth practices are directly related to the generation of some community health problems. Thus, the health culture is the sub-cultural entity in the culture which has been dealt in this study in an interdisciplinary perspective.

This study is an attempt to understand the health culture of the resettlement colony of Jahangirpuri and Bhalaswa as well. In order to understand, the cultural and social perception of health problem of the community a vast amount of qualitative data was collected from the community and the qualitative data strengthened and corroborated through quantitative data. The pertinent questions regarding health and health care structure of the colony, people were asked did the resident suffer or not in last two years, was there anybody still suffering, what step had been taken to mitigate the ailment, where they had gone for getting treated, who treated them, what was the result of the treatment, what all steps were taken by them to prevent illness, what did they do when they suffered of fever, what did they do when some one suffers from malaria, how did they conduct child birth in the community, what was done when a child suffered from diahorrea or dysentery, what was done in case of a patient suffering from tuberculosis, what measures were taken to prevent any kind of spread of communicable disease, what was done to comply with Family Welfare programme at the individual as well as at the family level, what are the types of local health care services people get, do they have their own type of health care practice and did they get any kind of ambulatory treatment etc. All the above mentioned queries helped gather a large amount of information regarding health and the health culture of the community.

It was observed that the people suffered of six broad categories of ailments i.e. minor, major, chronic, accident, psychological abnormalities and various types of allergy. The categorisation of these ailments were not arbitrarily done rather those cases were considered which were clinically confirmed. To understand the types of distribution of various kinds of ailment and its spatial distribution in the colony and the village, percentage distribution was calculated out of the main data gathered through interview schedule. Table 5.1 shows the distributions of the type of diseases (a broad categorisation has been done) people were suffering of.

The following distribution shows that the colony dwellers and the villagers were mainly suffering from chronic ailments (26%). The various chronic ailments were i.e. asthma, upper respiratory tract infections, skin disease, otitis media, depression, convulsion and fits. Second largest amount of incidence was of major ailments.

The major ailments were Tuberculosis, cancer, ailment of heart and kidney. It was observed that nearly ten percent of the people were having major ailment and majority of the people were suffering from T.B. Five percent of the people were suffering from minor ailments which comprised of ailment of Gastro-Intestinal Tracts, amoebic dysentery, hepatitis, rash of skin, diarrhoea, stomatitis, etc. Four percent of people were suffering from various accidents i.e. fracture of bone due to road accidents, cuts or bruise due to local skirmish or street brawls, burns due to accidental fire, or a fall from the staircase at home.

Table: 5.1

Distribution of Various Ailment Pattern of the Blocks (Jahangirpuri) and the Village Bhalasawa.

Block	*Minor*	*Major*	*Chronic*	*Accident*	*Psychic Ailment*	*Allergy*
A	4/45	5/45	8/45	1/45	-	-
B	1/42	3/42	12/42	-	-	-
C	3/49	2/49	24/49	-	-	-
E	2/47	7/47	10/47	1/47	2/47	-
I	2/	4/46	9/46	1/46	-	-
K	4/46	5/46	6/46	-	-	-
Village -	4/40	14/40	1/40	0	1/40	
Total	16/315 5%	30/315 9.5%	83/315 26%	4/315 1.2%	2/315 0.63%	1/315 0.31%

Only two percent psychic cases were seen and those were mainly Schizophrenia and neurosis due to shock (due to loss of near and dear or failure in business). A very small percentage of allergic cases were reported. Above mentioned diseases have been confirmed by the various institutes i.e. the local dispensary or the private practitioner and in some cases the treatment been given by the hospitals.

As per the general presumption, the economic status of individuals have certain bearing on the ailment and its type. It was found that fifty percent of the patients were poor (68/136). Whereas thirty eight percent of the sufferers of the total suffering population belonged to middle income group (52/136). And the study showed that the remaining twelve percent sufferer belonged to richer section of the population.

So far as the distribution of the type of ailments in respect to economic status was concerned, following trend been observed.

Table: 5.2

Distribution of Disease Pattern as per the Income Groups of the Resettlement and the Village Dwellers

Types of Ailment	*Poor*	*Middle*	*Rich*
Minor	7/136	12/136	2/136
	5.14%	8.82%	1.47%
Major	14/136	6/136	2/136
	10.29%	4.41%	1/47%
Chronic	43/136	23/136	1/136
	.73%	1.47%	.73%
Accident	2/136	1/136	1/136
	1.47%	.73%	.73%
Allergy	-	2/136	1/136
	-	1.47%	.73%
Total	67/136	46/136	23/136
	49.26%	33.82%	16.91%

Table 5.2 shows that the incidence of chronic ailment is high in all the income groups. Although, the main sufferers were the poor followed by the middle and the rich class of people respectively. The poor section of the population were mainly suffering of major ailments in comparison to the middle and the rich class of people. In cases of psychiatric, disorder no clear cut trend or pattern was seen, same was the case with accidents and cases of allergy (however, no trend or prevalence was studied in strict sense of the term).

It was also observed that the awareness of availability of health care institution amongst the people was quite prominent, so they visited various health care organisations, but it was also found that they showed reluctance some times to go to these institutions due to various domestic and economic constraints and they did stop going to these places when they did not find any kind of relief.

Table: 5.3

Visits of the Colony Dwellers and Villagers to Various Health Care Institutions

Block	*Visit to Private*	*Visit to Govt.*	*Visit to Both*	*Home Remedy*	*Natural Cure*
A	7/45	8/45	17/45	1/45	24/45
	(15.5)	(13)	(38)	(2)	(55.5)
B	6/42	2/42	10/42	0/42	25/42
	(14)	(5)	(34)	(0)	(59.5)
C	11/49	8/49	7/49	1/49	20/49
	(11)	(11)	(19)	(2)	(36)
E	5/47	5/47	9/47	1/47	17/47
	(11)	(11)	(19)	(2)	(36)
I	5/46	3/46	8/36	1/46	28/46
	(11)	(6.5)	(17)	(2)	(61)
K	4/46	1/46	8/46	0/46	33/46
	(9)	(2)	(17)	(0)	(72)
Village	6/40	4/40	8/40	02/40	21/40
	(15)	(10)	(20)	(5)	(52.5)
Total	44/315	29/315	67/315	6/315	169/315
	(13.96)	(9.20)	(20.28)	(1.9)	(53.65)

The Table 5.2, showed that the chronic cases were quite high, as a result, opinion about the performance of the various health institution were not good. The awareness about the various dispensaries and their efficacy of treatment were made known to people by the neighbours rather than by the staffs or doctors. Regarding any national programme they came to know more from the media i.e. radio and T.V. and to a large extent these informations combined with urgency to get cured lead people to take treatment. Table 5.3 showed the patterns of visit to the various health care organisations by the residents undertaken during their ailment.

It was found that fifty three to fifty four percent of the people did not visit to any one of the health care institutions rather they believed in natural cure and remedy. Fourteen percent of the resettlement and the village dwellers visited to private dispensaries. Whereas, only nine percent of the people had visited to government hospitals or dispensaries. However, it may seem paradoxical that the people visited to private clinics were more whereas they visited government dispensary lesser number of times. The prominent reasons given for such behaviour was:

- The patient gets more sympathetic and patience hearing from the private doctor. He empathises with patients.
- The doctors gave better medicine as he charged for it, so the efficacy was more in private medication.
- The patient did not waste time by sitting and loose wage for the day while waiting for check up.
- The doctors could be approached any time, as per patients covenience.
- The doctor made visit to patients houses during emergency.

It was also told by the patients that the government doctors were no less competent in treating skills or in their technical know-how to diagnose. The rude behaviour of staffs, including that of the doctors were unappreciable combined with chronic shortage of medicine.

It was also revealed from the study that around twenty percent of the people of this area visited both to the private and government dispensaries. The people who had visited both to private and government dispensaries were not particular about any kind of special treatment rather they had visited to the practitioner as per their urgency and convenience.

So far as home remedy was concerned the practice of such remedy was almost negligible. It was found that only two percent of the people believed in such practices. It became very clear that amongst the resettlers and the villagers clientel of allopathic and ayurvedic medicines were common whereas the traditional medicine was almost non-existent in both the communities. The main reason was that the people were much interested about the scientifically established treatment pattern and much more tangible and prompt effect of the medicine taken.

The cure by traditional means was equally inappreciable in the poor and the richer section of the population. To know more about such practice one poor rickshaw puller was contacted. Hari Om. A dweller of Block C, was earning his livelihood by pulling rickshaw and supported his family of six single handedly. He was asked why did not he take home remedy during ailment, he replied that

> .... he knows that if he uses home remedy for cure of ills then he would save lot of money which otherwise goes to the doctor. But, he also knows that he cannot carry out so many do's and don'ts of the home remedy. in which case he will put himself and his family members in much more trouble. Moreover, he realises that many things he does not know exactly and has forgotten many things due to passage of time and lack of practice. Moreover, staying for long duration in this colony he got cut off from his previous village life, where he was getting a lot of ideas from fellow villagers and elderlies of the village about home remedy.

It is evident from the above mentioned conversation that the allopathic way of cure is more time tested and popular due to its higher rate of cure in comparison to home remedy, in case of most of the treatments. It also brought out one more factor that, the people were getting alienated gradually from the pre-existing health care practices due of lack of knowledge and know-how. On the other hand, more and more Allopathic and Ayurvedic care were sought after by the resettlers for treatment.

And, so, it was obvious that within few years people in an urban setting like Jahangirpuri or in a village like Bhalasawa would forget home remedies or traditional health care practices completely.

An old fellow from poorer section of the community was asked about the dying art of home remedy and how it was being practised. The respondent Babu Lal a hexagenerian said in the following words,

> .... he gives massage of a particular mix of turmeric and oil in different proportion as per the age and severity of the casualty viz; fracture of bone or dislocation of bone. The dislocation of bone is easily fixed by him. He gives the patient a particular type of jerk and places the bone in proper position. Thereafter, he calls the patient at various intervals i.e. three days. seven days, ten days etc. Depending upon the severity of the case for complete recovery, he gives them home made oil for the purpose of massage...

He was again asked that, does he know any thing else, he replied in affirmative and said the following,

> .... he has made some medicine. which he prescribes to the women having complain of irreguler mences, heavy bleeding for quite some times. and such

cases. who have been prescribed cleaning (D.N.C.). if they visit him. he gives them certain dose of his medicine and that certainly cures those ladies.

The scholár asked one of the aged ladies (mother) of the same family that does she also practice any one of the skill of Babu Lal. The mother of Babu Lal said the following things (she was an eighty year old lady),

> .... She advises about known native taboos to the young ladies, when they conceive, in terms of what they should eat or not eat at the time of pregnancy. She also ask them not to take too much spicy food besides not to take too much sour, hot stuff or oily things. And after they deliver they are advised to take Sonth, Goondh, laddoos because these are highly nutritive, rich in fat and carbohydrate. Moreover. she, advises the young mothers to take milk at least 250 gms a day along with those special diets....

These facts made it clear that as of now the practice of such therapy is confound among the elderlies only. Moreover, it was also a kind of family tradition, one cannot find the practice of this treatment in such houses where the elderlies did not know about it.

Naresh Kumar, a thirty year old man from poorer section of E-Block was asked by the scholar that why did he opt for private care instead of free government health care which was available in this colony.

> .... he is a daily wage earner, working in a factory, where he earns hundred rupees per day and he looks after five persons with that earning. If he goes to government dispensary then he will have to stand in queue and waste at least two hours to take one or two tablets, and those tablets do not prove effective as well. and ultimately he goes to private practitioner only to get more efficacious treatment. In government dispensary, they (all the staffs and doctors) treat them like animal they talk to rich people very nicely. He does not mind spending money and getting treated rather than wasting the whole day and wage for free health care.

He was again asked that who does he think should visit to the government dispensaries. He replied:

> .... he thinks those who are rich because such patients can get good preferential treatment. Besides, those who have lot of time at their disposal and are ready to be treated as per the wish of the doctors....

This shows that the people who visited the government organisation were visiting under compulsion and those who could afford, otherwise most of the people did not mind spending some money and to go for private treatment.

Similarly, a head of the family was asked, (who preferred to visit to the government dispensary). Ram Dayal a clerk in Delhi Administration He had five members in his family, was asked that ...."why did he go to government dispensaries when most of the people did not have any faith in it, moreover, they complained about the mis-conduct and bad behaviour of the staff...." He replied.

> .... he was a card holder of Delhi Administration dispensary and he was authorised to visit any one of the Delhi Administration dispensaries of the colony his office deduct a particular amount from his salary towards his family's health care. Besides, whenever he fell sick and was not in a position to go to office for couple of days he was treated and given fitness certificate to join on duty without loss of leave or pay. But he also told that it was two way process, if somebody is looking for extra benefit, he have to earn it.

He was further asked about extra benefit and two way process, He told,

> ".... he was in horticulture division and the doctors were interested in good gardens, so he managed seeds and grafted saplings for them and gaves it to them as and when the doctors requested. Moreover, his son used to go to doctors residence to teach their child free of charge."
>
> So, Ram Dayal is liked by many doctors of the local dispensaries...

It was clear from the above narrations that those who had gone out of the way to grow personal relationship they only reaped the fruit of good consultancy and treatment. In other words, the system which apparently looked absolutely contractual and unbias is rather based on personal equation.

Many residents visit to both the government and the private institution. Mr. Banwari Lal of Block-A, who also happened to be a worker in Birla Mills and was entitled to get treated under the Employee State Insurance (ESI) scheme, preferred to take private care as well. His explaination for doing so is given as:

> ".... as he was entitled to visit government dispensary so he used to

> visit there, as and when he needed any treatment. But of late he had taken a decision. Whenever, he or any one of his family members needed treatment, went to private practitioner, (if the ailment was not of grave nature). Because, the treatment given in the private clinic was much more faster and one need not waste time in the name of treatment. But, whenever he realised that inspite of few days of treatment, the private doctor was unable to control or treat then he visited to ESI, there was provision to get treated at the expense of the employer"

The scholar asked that, why does he switch over from one practitioner to other, will it not harm the patient, he emphatically said "no". And minor ailments should be treated in private clinic to get quick remedy.

The above case clearly shows that the people of the colony were judicious in their own way, because they did not prefer to waste their time and energy for small things, whereas they did visit the government health care institution when they knew that the private treatment was highly expensive.

A majority was found to be believer in natural cure, such beliefs were manifestation of various factors i.e. paucity of money, lack of time, loss of faith on practitioners. Mrs. Vimla of Block-E, who was also reluctant to get cured due to lack of money. She said that she was feeling weak and dizzy for the last seven months but was not taking any medicine, she further said

> .... she did not want to take any treatment because she thought. she would be alright in natural course. as her mother-in-law died seven months ago, so, she was doing extra work which led to weakness and dizziness, but. nothing else.

But it was clear from the conversation with the lady that she was extremely weak and sick therefore she needed immediate care and medical attention. After detailed conversation with the lady, it was found that she was not able to go to doctor who would charge for consultancy and will prescribe such medicines for which she would spend substantial amount of money through her nose which she could not afford. Her Husband was poor rickshaw puller who was not in a position to pay money for treatment or medication.

It was found that the perception of a disease and its meaning was different, in different income groups. As it was realised from the above example of Vimla that her ailment was a secondary issue for herself, as she knew that her treatment meant an extra expenditure for the family.

On the contrary, Banwari Lal, the mill worker could afford to go to the private practitioner at the first instance but he did not visit the government organisation or the government doctor, he visited only when he found that the situation was deteriorating instead of improving. This showed that the meaning and perception of the ailment for him is not monetary gain or loss; rather it was largely efficacy of the treatment. He was not interested to waste time in queue in the name of free health care treatment.

While considering the cases of poor T.B. patients of the colony, it was found that the diagnosed cases of RBTB hospital were being really treated well for the first three months of the treatment, whereas the situation changed largely afterwards, when the patients were advised for follow-up treatment. Some of the patients took it and some did not as some were not in a position to go again and again to get their medicine even if it was available in E Block dispensary. Because many a time it happened that the stock of medicine got exhausted and they had to go twice or thrice there for the medicine (because the patients were not in a position to purchase the medicine of their own). Ultimately, it resulted in discontinuity and relapse of the disease. It meant that even if they were able to perceive this dreadful disease they were unable to do anything. Moreover, the recovering patients needed adequate diet, which was mostly not possible for the family members to provied in most of the cases.

It was also necessary to know the reason of liking or disliking of the government dispensaries by the colony dwellers in order to get the picture of, level of state intervention and the role it is playing to maintain the health status of the people. The following table gives the distribution of reasons for frequenting to government dispensaries.

Two factors became very clear that irrespective of income groups and class the patients and the people of this area were concerned for too much delay and wastage of time in the queue. And secondly the efficacy of the treatment of the government organisation was also a metter of concern. The other two factors which were affecting the treatment pattern of the government dispensaries was the non-easy accessibility and lack of fast as well as prompt emergency care. Every individual asked for betterment of the emergency care in the government dispensaries.

Table: 5.4

Reasons of Visiting to Various Health Care Institutions by different Income Groups

Various Reasons of Visit	*Poor*	*Middle*	*Rich*
Due to Easy Accessibility	7 (2.2)	10 (3.17)	7 (2.2)
During Emergency Care	12 (3.80)	17 (8.57)	10 (3.17)
Due to Efficacy	30 (18.0)	55 (17.40)	30 (9.6)
To save Time	34 (10.79)	34 (10.73)	6 (1.90)
To get Preferential Treatment	1 (0.3)	-	20 (6.34)
For Door Step Care	-	10 (3.17)	-
To get Free Govt. Care	4 (1.26)	10 (3.17)	-
Total	(30)95/315	(52)166/315	(18)54/315

It was essential to know the status of the mother and child, besides the status of expecting and the lactating mother of the colony. As the category has been designated as "vulnerable age group", so understanding of the health culture of these people becomes an equally important task.

The Infrastructure of Maternal and Child Health care (MCH)

In the MCD. dispensaries, the lady doctors were mostly posted to look after every aspects of mother and childs health. The Auxiliary Nurse Midwives (ANM) were primarily meant to carry out all the MCH activities along with the doctors but they were mainly engaged in carrying out the family welfare activity. They were keen to complete their target of sterilisation as the target was directly linked with increments, promotions and various other incentives. Even the class -IV staff of the dispensaries were involved in completing the targets in tacit manner because they were also given incentives of various kinds. Moreover, they had been asked to promote the concept of contraceptives by which the desired couple protection rate could be achieved. So far as the delivery of child was concerned, it was either carried out at home or at hospital, mostly in Babu Jagjivan Ram Memorial Hospital, the centres did not have any facilities of beds even though they had expertise. The expecting mothers in any case at least visited once to the dispensary for a check up as it was being given free of cost. But the visit to dispensary during the hours of delivery was a remote possibility so the ANMs or the trained dais of the dispensary were requested to visit to the house for the delivery. Although, the doctors of the centre told that the para-medical staff were supposed to attend the call duties, even if they come to know by any means, unfortunately the reality was that the family member of the expecting lady used to coax and cajole these ANM's or Dais to attend the delivery at their residents and gave handsome amount for the same.

During conversations with Tara Devi an experienced mother, it was quite clear that in her first two deliveries she had called *ANMs*. She told,

> "…. during her first delivery, she was bit scared and she had no elderly to look after so, she was advised by her husband that she must consult the centre people instead of any neighbour and they were new to this place as well . The start of labour pain followed by ANM's arrival from the dispensary as she came and conducted the delivery charged Rs. 151/-and she told that she will not accept any thing less than that, so they were forced to give that amount. Second time after two years one of the ANM was called to conduct the delivery and and son was born before she arrived so she insisted for Rs.101/- and one piece of sari. As they wanted to bargain on one of the items, she was vexed so, Tara Devi conceded to her demand…."

She was asked, "did not she know that they were not to be paid because it was a part of their duty"… She replied,

> …. She knew but ANMs are very obstinate and nothing is going to happen if the complaint is made against them. Moreover, nobody wanted to spoil the mood at that point of time…, and she also said that during her third and fourth child she did not consult any one of them because she did not want to spend huge amounts, on the contrary she had called one of the local dais who was very happy with the amount given to her i.e. Rs. 51/- on each occasion. Besides, after two issues if any body goes for third or fourth one, the *dai* of the centre often threatens for sterilisation and she would take up the matter to the higher-ups as well, in order to sterlise both the spouses. Whereas the local *dai* does not bully, the only problem of local dai is they mostly belong to lower caste viz. *bhangi* (sweeper). But local *dai* also comes after delivery for massage even up to three days, in complicated deliveries she even comes for five days to carry out the

> massage. And she gladly accepts whatever amount is given. Whereas the government dai never comes to do massage at the most she visits the next day to check the mother and child. Some of these local *dais* do wash and clean dirty clothes after delivery as well. But they charge very reasonable amount for washing clothes of delivery and post delivery. Many of these local *dais* are so good that they even come before delivery at times for giving massage without charging extra....

On enquiring, about the prophylactic doses for the expecting mothers of the colony. Mrs. Nirmal of Block-E told about the dosages of Iron and Foilic acid besides, the Tetanus toxoide, in the following words.

> .... they do not believe in prophylactic measure, they do not believe in any tablets, they give good food and milk, so the ladies need not take Vitamin tablets, so far as the injection of Tetanus Toxoid is concerned and its course of three injections. it is simply money making business of the doctors she told. She delivered seven children neither she took any injection nor did any of her child was given any injection. And her daughter-in-law was also expecting and she advised her to not to get any injection. She was sure that nothing will happen....

It was also observed that some of the enlightened mothers did take their child for injection immediately after the birth.

Table 5.4 shows that only fifty percent of the pre-term women were taking prepartum checkup. Subsequently, it was also studied amongst the colony women that whether the dosage of Tetanus Toxoide (T.T.) were being administered to all the income groups equally or not.

Table 5.5 shows that there is no remarkable difference between utilisers and non utilisers within the poorer community, so far as the administrator of T.T. was concerned. In case of middle income group, it was seen that majority of the women did not go for T.T injection.

It was also found from the study that cent percent rich people had taken the injection of T.T., such high coverage aroused curosity regarding the way of coverage. On asking Kanta Devi of Block-B, regarding her perception who happened to be a mother of two children and belonging to rich class, why rich women were getting cent percent coverage but not the poor. She replied in the following words.

Table: 5.5

Distribution of Dosage of Tetanus Toxoide taken by the Pregnant Women of Various Income Groups of the Study Population

Income Group	*T.T.Taken*	*T.T. not Taken*	*Taken Could not Recollect*	*Total*
Poor	43(45.0)	47(50.0)	5(5.0)	95
Middle	65(39.0)	95(57.1)	6(3.9)	166
Rich	54(100.0)	-	-	54
Total	162/315	142/315	11/315	315

...so far as she thinks about the reason for cent percent coverage amongst the rich for vaccination i.e. watching and listening in T.V. and radio about the benefits of the injection. But the poor do not have time to listen because they have to devote their time and energy for earning to square of meals. Whereas, that is not the case with the rich. Secondly, they do not understand even if they see or listen about it because they are uneducated and most of them are illiterate. So, she thinks in the given condition it become duty of the centre staff particularly of the ANMs and the *dais* to inform these people (the poor) about the benefits of these injections....

Table: 5.6

Distribution of Various Income Group According to the Preference of Place of Delivery

E.Class	*Delivery at Home*	*Centre*	*Govt. Hospital*	*Nursing Home*	*G.H. & NH*	*Could Not Recollect*	*Total*
Poor	58(18.4)	9(8.8)	14(4.4)	3(.9)	6(1.9)	5(1.5)	95
Middle	53(16.8)	9(2.8)	16(5.0)	5(1.5)	72(22.8)	11(3.4)	166
Rich	46(14.6)	2(0.63)	-	6(1.9)	-	-	54
Total	157/315	20/315	30/315	14/315	78/315	16/315	315

This demostrated that there were some communication gap between the poor and the staff of the dispensary or for that matter even between the hospital and the target women, (where these women had gone for delivery). The poor and the middle income group did not get access to the services of the centre. Only a small fraction of the respondents could not recollect whether they had taken any injection or not because in those cases deliveries were carried out at home only.

In the present study, it was also found out that which were the agencies in which the expecting mothers preferd to go for delivery.

Table 5.6 shows that maximum home delivery took place amongst the poorer section of the population. And particularly amongst the poorer Muslims, home delivery was too high. The scholar asked one of the poor Bengali Muslim of C-Block, Mrs. Amina that .....why did she opt for home delivery.... She replied

> ...in her village in Bengal she had elderly ladies who were ever ready to help them during delivery period, and the delivery was conducted in Janana or ladies chamber where no one else could go during delivery.
>
> Only husband was allowed during the delivery. In other words, they had *"Pardah"* (exclusive room), and in the villages the lady doctors were only permitted within the house for check up but no one else of the hospital or dispensary were allowed. Given that background, how all of a sudden could she change the custom. In the beginning, (exclusive room) they had some problems in Jahangirpuri without any elderly lady. But over the period of time, a Muslim elderly lady from Midnapur district of West Bengal arrived and she helps in deliveries. She is an expert in the art of carrying out delivery so she only helps the expecting mothers. Moreover, there is no question of payment, because as per the Quaran she is doing a holy act in the name of Allah, so she will never make it a business or charge for the delivery.

From the above conversation, it became clear that the people of the poorer strata were unable to pay and so they did not go for private clinics for delivery.

But, by and large it was observed that all the women of this group were in favour of delivery at home. But the order of preference for delivery at home decreased from the poor to rich group. It revealed from the study that the poor groups and the middle class had utilised the facility of maternity centre. As in Jahangirpuri, there were no centres for conducting delivery, so the cases were conducted at Kingsway Camp maternity centre initially. However, of late the deliveries were conducted at Babu Jagjivan Ram Memorial Hospital. But the rich visited private maternity centre during the delivery of child. But the visit to nursing home by the rich people for delivery of child was also not uncommon. Quite contrary to such practice it was found that the poor had rarely gone to the nursing home for delivery. It was obvious that they refrained from going to nursing home because it was beyond their means.

So far as the delivery in the government or private centres was concerned, it was found that maximum number of middle income group women visited to both the private and the government institutions for delivery. While majority of the poor were not in a position to get their delivery conducted in private centres.

In order to know that after the child was born how many survived and how many died, informations were gathered from various income groups. Such informations showed direct relation of child survival in relation to income of the family.

Table: 5.7

Distribution of Number of Birth, Number of Child Survived, Still Birth and Abortion in Various Income Groups

Income Group	*Total No. of Birth*	*No. of Children Died*	*Still Birth*	*Abortion*
Poor	450	30	22	20
Middle	400	15	8	5
Rich	378	10	5	3
Total	1228 (4.47)	55 (2.85)	35 (2.2)	28

It is clear from the Table 5.7 that in all, the poor loose more children in comparison to the middle and richer section of the population. As the table shows that in the poor income group the still birth rate was higher than that of the middle and the rich class. The largest number of abortions were also reported amongst the poor. The cases of abortion were reported minimum amongst the richer section, whereas it was relatively more in the middle income group.

The reason of higher rate of child death, still birth and rate of abortion was highlighted by a lady of poorer section from block-I, she, herself happened to be mother of five children. She told,

> ...they are poor people and so they could not take the child to the doctor and could not afford time and money, if at all they managed to take the newly born to the doctor they could not afford medicine due to lack of money. Similarly, if the now born happend to be fourth or fifth issue and the

> family did not have any male child then no parents give attention to the newly born female child. If the child survives it is absolutely her own luck...

The female who had abortion or still birth in Jahangirpuri or in the village, it was observed that mostly the ladies were weak and they were also over burdened with heavy domestic work which lead to various complication during delivery or even lead to miscarriage. In most of the still births, it was observed that mothers who conceived had to bear one or orther type of trouble till the delivery. Another factor which came out glaringly the death of female child was more than the male and not much carcern were raised about it.

The above statements clearly proves that most of their problem were due to poor socio-economic life style, the husbands were not in a position to give any extra care or attention to their wives after conception and during and after delivery as well as. The ladies in these communities were over burdened with daily domestic chores. Whereas, in case of middle and the rich section this was not the problem.

One of the ladies of the poor economic group called, Laxmi was asked..... "does she give something else other than milk to the new born"... who was a mother of four children and the fourth was still suckling

> "Most of their children were breast fed for a long period, they did not get sufficient solid food as substitute, often the child were fed on breast milk. She further said breast feeding was a common pehnomena amongst the poor and the middle section but the rich were not used to long breast feeding as they could afford other foods.

The lady was again asked ... "does she give colustrum to her child"...She said :

> Colustrum is very bad thing that is not milk and if it is given to the child, then the child is invariably going to suffer. That is first of all yellow in colour and viscid in nature because that is spoiled milk. It was rather ceremoniously discarded and after that only the child is allowed to suckle.

In continuation to breast feeding the lady told,

> moreover, they knew that they could not give any thing better to their child which will improve their child's health, so, breast feeding is essential as long as possible. These days it is too costly to purchase those powders

> which are given to rich man's child. They could not afford those powder milk but they could give bread (double roti), biscuits and some times *banana* (meshed) to their child, and when they could not give *banana* then they gave boiled potato....

The above mentioned situation clearly explained that the mothers of poorer economic section knew about extra breast feed, but they were handicapped due to economic constraints. And the child mainly grows in an adverse socio-economic life conditions where his life expectency become less.

An old lady of seventy form Block-I, was asked that... what sort of do's and don'ts advised to her daughter-in-laws, when they gave birth to child. She told,

> "First of all she advises them not to handle too much of heavy things during conception as well as after delivery. The ladies after delivery were not allowed to go out minimum for three days and maximum for seven days. Moreover, the new born was also not taken out of house. Strict advices to daughters and daughter-in-law were given to feed their child exclusively on breast. She also advised her daughters and daughter-in-law to take as much ghee as they can. She also stressed that they must take turmeric, in their diet also"....

Table: 5.8

Distribution of Post Partum Rest Taking Pattern of the Women as of Three Income Groups

Income Group	*5-10d*	*10-15d*	*15-20d*	*20-25d*	*25-30d*	*30-40d*	*40-60d*	*60+d*	*Can't Say*
Poor	18	12	5	7	15	20	10	7	1
	(18.9)	(12.6)	(5.2)	(7.3)	(15.7)	(21)	(10.5)	(7.3)	(1.0)
Middle	17	15	7	8	35	48	14	8	14
	(10.2)	(9.0)	(4.2)	(4.8)	(21.0)	(28.9)	(8.4)	(4.8)	(8.4)
Rich	16	8	3	3	1	6	9	3	5
	(29.6)	(14.8)	(5.5)	(5.5)	(1.8)	(11.1)	(16.6)	(5.5)	(9.2)
Total	51	35	15	18	51	74	33	18	20

These customs also show that the older generation ladies were aware of the need of more fat or carbohydrate diet which was required in plenty during and after pregnancy. Moreover, the combination of milk with turmeric was a combination of complete food with antibiotics, which proved very nutritive for mother. The post partum rest was meant to regain her normalcy to start the routine activities again.

The number of days the mothers staying in bed or taking rest has been found out in the present study and the time duration for rest of women among different income strata have been also found out.

Table 5.8 shows that as per convention and tradition the women were mostly in favour of rest for period of 30 to 40 days in the post partum stage but they also admitted that given the present situation one can not enjoy that much rest. The middle and the poor section said that they did not to really enjoy rest due to work pressure.

But it was also observed that majority of the women could atleast take 5 to 10 days of rest after delivery.

Whatever, the customs might be it was clear from the conversation with the women of the area that irrespective of religion or caste, they were of the opinio. that such long rest was unaffordable under present conditions. And some of the women particularly the working ones said it would be wastage of time and money. Because, if they did not work, their income would go down and would face severe consequances. However, a clear cut paradox can be seen in the practice of post partum rest custom, because most of the working women were from the poor and the middle strata, and they were supposed to earn on one hand and on the other they were also to rear child and look after themselves. As the former act was more essential so the ladies sacrificed the latter by justifying the former as useless custom.

In the same light in the present study an effort was made to know the feeding practices of the mothers of the area. The duration of feeding was equally important because it was directly connected with the growth and development of the child.

It is clear from the Table 5.9 that nearly thirty eight percent of the women breast fed their child from one and a half years to two years, or in other words more than one third of the women were following the prolonged feeding practice. The next largest group was one who breast fed from six months to one year. Castes, religious and income group were no way impedement to the prolonged breast feeding. There was a group who practised breast feeding from one year to one and a half years. Less than ten percent fed less than six months. Less than ten percent fed, more than three years. It was clear from the study that poor and the middle section of women continued breast feeding for longer period. Whereas, the rich did not breast feed their child for much longer period.

Table: 5.9

Distribution of Breast Feeding Duration of the Mothers Income Strata

Income Group	*1-6m*	*6-12m*	*1-1½yr*	*1½yr-2yr*	*2-3yr*	*3+*	*Can't Say*
Poor	10	20	15	35	14	-	1
	(10.5)	(21.0)	(15.7)	(36.8)	(14.7)		(1.0)
Middle	10	22	18	60	20	15	21
	(6.0)	(13.2)	(10.8)	(36.1)	(12.0)	(9.0)	(12.6)
Rich	4	14	9	23	-	3	1
	(7.4)	(25.9)	(16.6)	(42.5)	-	(5.5)	(1.8)
Total	24/315	56/315	42/315	118/315	24/315	18/315	23/315

In the present study, an attempt was also made to find out the beginning of weaning for the new borns.

The following table shows the frequency distribution of the weaning period among the three different economic strata.

Table 5.10 shows that the concept of extra food other than the breast milk started at the onset of very first month and mothers started extra feed right from the first month to six months after birth. And nearly fifty four percent practised extra breast feed from one month to six month after birth. The scholar wanted to know from one of the mothers of the middle income category women what extra breast feed is given to the child, who has not crossed first six months of his life, but he is more than one month old. The question was put to Shanti Devi, mother of three children from block-K she replied in the following words.

> .....They start giving the child some extra feed due to various reasons i.e. they were told at the centre or in the hospital during stay that they must give something other than breast milk from the first fourth month of the birth. Many a time mother did not have flow of milk for more than a

> month or two then, it became highly essential to give extra milk. Mothers doing job could not get adequate time to suckle and subsequently they were forced to start extra milk from second or third month onwards, besides, a very few amongst them felt that the powder milk is equally or more nutritive than mothers milk....

Table: 5.10

The Trend of Weaning in the Three Income Groups

Income Group	*1m-6m*	*6m-1yr.*	*1yr.-2yr.*	*2yr.-3yr.*	*3yr.-*	*No Weaning*
Poor	30 (31.5)	35 (36.8)	5 (5.2)	8 (8.4)	5 (5.2)	12 (12.6)
Middle	97 (58.4)	55 (33.1)	10 (6.0)	1 (.60)	-	3 (1.8)
Rich	42 (77.7)	9 (16.6)	3 (5.5)	-	-	-
Total	169/315	19/315	18/315	9/315	5/315	15/315

When asked; "what type of extra feed given to the child".... the lady replied

> .....they mostly gave their child the canned powder milk, viz. Nestle or Glaxo. And those who could not afford powder milk they generally gave diluted cows milk or goat milk because that was easy for digestion rather than buffalo milk and those who started extra feed did not give anything else other than extra milk at least up to the age of six months.....

This also proved that majority of mothers remained confined to extra breast milk during weaning period but the child was not given meshed vegetable or fruit or stew of pulses. Other notable feature was some have started weaning their child at the age of six months to one year after birth. Both the middle and the poor section of the population followed the above trend, while the richer section of the people were not so late in weaning rather they start right on the first month. So far the weaning practice of rich people were concerned they gave everything (food items) which the middle or the poor could not afford due to economic constraints i.e. meshed vegetable, meshed fruits, fruit juice and the powder milk. It was clear from the study that eighty five percent of the mothers started to wean their child at the age of one month and at the most they started as late as one year. It was found that only ten percent of mothers, started weaning after one year of age.

To verify the concept of "larger the lactation period lesser the chances of conception" question were put to ladies in this area and that yielded a mixed and varied response.

Table 5.11 shows that the belief was connected with a particular income group very strongly.

Table: 5.11

Trend of Believe Pattern in Relation to Prolong Breast Feeding Prevents Pregnancy

Income Group	*I Agree*	*I Don't Agree*	*Don't Know*	*Heard Only*
Poor	25	20	45	5
	(26.3)	(21.0)	(47.3)	(13.2)
Middle	34	25	99	8
	(20.4)	(16.0)	(59.6)	(4.8)
Rich	30	20	0	4
	(55.5)	(37.0)	-	(4.2)
Total	89/315	65/315	144/315	17/315

The Table 5.11 shows that nearly equal number of people have agreed and disagreed about the concept in all the different income groups. Few respondents categorically refused about the concept. Mrs. Manorama an woman from richer section was asked that does she endorse this concept, if, not then why, she replied,

> she used to believe in this concept as her mother-in-law also used to tell her about this concept, so she and her husband were quite, confident and after having the third child they thought that, as long as the third child will be breast fed she can not conecive. But, after two months she realised that she conceived again. But as she told the same to her mother-in-law and to her husband as well, they never took it seriously and told her that she is unnecessarily fussy about it, she can't conceive. So, she did not go for medical check up, but at that time her youngest one was still suckling. And when they visited to the doctor, doctor refused to do abortion and told her that she was too weak to undergo, Medically Terminated Pregnancy (MTP) and she had to accept the child as gods gift.....

Forty six percent of the mothers were not sure about the belief.

They said very categorically that they never heard about it. A mere five percent of the people said they heard only, but did not know anything about it. One clear cut distinction was seen that the rich people by and large agreed or disagreed to this concept but did not say that they did know very clearly about the concept.

Milk consumption is one of the major markers of nutritive intake of a child, so, in the present study it was also assessed that how much milk a child consumed per day.

The following table mentioned shows clearly that the tea intake in the community and in the village was very high. Thirty six percent of the people were taking tea or in other words more than one third of the people were consuming tea. It also became clear from the study that the tea consumption was high in the poor and middle income group. A comparison between the middle and the poor, showed that the middle strata children (48%) consumed tea where as amongst the poor nearly thirty two percent consumed tea.

Table: 5.12

Amount of Milk Consumption Per Day Per Child of Different Strata

Income Group	*100g*	*100-250g*	*250-500g*	*500-750g*	*750g*	*No Intake*	*Tea & Milk*	*Tea Only*
Poor	17 (17.8)	25 (26.3)	5 (5.2)	-	-	10 (10.5)	8 (8.4)	30 (31.5)
Middle	20 (12.0)	38 (22.8)	15 (9.0)	8 (4.8)	5 (3.0)	- (4.8)	-	80 (48.1)
Rich	10 (18.5)	20 (37.0)	10 (18.5)	4 (7.4)	6 (11.1)	-	-	6 (7.4)
Total	39/315	83/315	30/315	12/315	11/315	12/315	8/315	114/115

So far as the milk and tea consumption were concerned, it was found that only poor consumed both tea and milk, in irregular proportion (less milk and more tea). Similarly, ten percent of the poor did not take any thing, neither milk nor tea. And nearly five percent of the rich could take milk or tea. So far as heavy consumption of milk (more than 750gm) per day was concerned, it was found that three percent of the middle class could afford that much, whereas eleven percent of rich could afford that amount of milk. But no poor could afford that much. Even no poor could go for 500gm of milk per day. Only middle and rich took more than 500gm of milk per day.

The study showed that a larger section of the people of all income group could afford between 100gm to 250gm milk a day. The order of consumption of milk was, poor twenty six percent, twenty three percent middle class and thirty seven percent of the rich consumed 100gm to 250gm milk per day respectively.

This type of variation in consumption of milk to a large extent could be attributed to the economic disparity of the people of that area. At the same time tea consumption is more of addiction and a good replacement to consumption of milk. As few mothers of the children told that, they could not afford initially milk for all the children which ultimately resulted in regular dislike for milk of the children. While, the children got tea as and when they desired.

Immunisation Practices of the Community

Immunisation is one of the most talked of national programme as this is important to prevent the life of many mothers and neo-nate. In order to know the immunisation status of the community, the queries were made and the varied responses have been gathered.

The following table shows that amongst the poor nearly seventy percent have taken vaccination. It was also observed from the study that nearly eleven percent of the families in the poor category could not get their two or more children vaccinated. And it was also found that nearly eight percent of households in the poor community did not go for any kind of vaccination. Six percent could not recollect whether they got their children vaccinated or not.

Amongst the middle class it was found almost seventy percent of the children got vaccinated. Whereas nearly fourteen percent of the middle class children did not go for any sort of vaccinations. It was also found that twelve percent of the families did not vaccinate at least one of their children.

In case of rich, it was found that eighty three percent of children got vaccinated. The study also showed that nine percent of the children were not vaccinated. And seven percent of the mothers could not recollect that whether they got their children vaccinated or not.

Table: 5.13

Distribution of Vaccinated and Non-Vaccinated Children in three Income Groups.

Income Groups	*All Vaccinated*	*two or more Vaccinated*	*One to be Vaccinated*	*No Vaccine*	*Could not Recollect*
Poor	65 (68.42%)	10 (10.52%)	6 (6.31%)	8 (8.42%)	6 (6.31%)
Middle	113 (68%)	5 (3%)	20 (12%)	23 (13.85%)	5 (3%)
Rich	45 (83%)	5 (9.25%)	-	-	4 (7.4%)
Total	223/315	20/315	26/315	31/315	15/315

But, it revealed that seventy one percent of the children on average got vaccinated in all the three strata. The reasons of failure to vaccinate the child was attributed to the shortage of time of the parents which made it difficult for the daily wage earner to take their child to the dispensary or maternity centre again and again. They said that it was very difficult for them (daily wage carners) to visit the centre repeatedly, because the vaccines were not found at the centre due to irregular supply of the vaccine at given point of time as a result vaccination was not done in a single go.

The unscrupulous staff did harass at times the poor resettlement colony dwellers or the villagers in order to get some money, which he is not entitled to demand for vaccinating the children.

It was also observed that in some cases the children have been vaccinated by unsterilised needles which ultimately resulted in some kind of complication amongst the children. Subsequently, that lead to a great deal of apathy in the minds of the people of the area towards vaccination.

In order to know more about vaccination system in the colony and the village it was equally important to know about the various agencies which were responsible to carry out the job of vaccination. Information regarding the places of vaccination was gathered from the residents of the colony.

It was found from the study that almost eighty percent of the poor were taking their children for vaccination to government dispensary. Whereas, five percent of the children were taken to various organisations for vaccination.

Table 5.14

Trend of Availing the Vaccination from Different Health Care Institutions Among the Three Strata

Income Group	*Govt. Dispensary*	*Govt. Hospital*	*Pvt. Hospital*	*General Practioner*	*Pvt. & Govt..*	*No Recollection*
Poor	75 (79%)	5 (5.26%)	- -	5 (5.26%)	5 (5.25%)	5 (5.2%)
Middle	100 (60%)	9 (5.42%)	-	15 (9%)	10 (6%)	32 (19.27%)
Rich	32 (59.25%)	-	68 (14.81%)	3 (5.55%)	7 (13%)	4 (7.4%)
Total	207/315	14/315	8/315	23/315	23/315	41/315

In case of middle strata, sixty percent children were taken to dispensaries for vaccination, followed by nine percent of the children to both government and private organisation. Whereas, it was found that only five to six percent were taken to government and private doctors as well. Almost nineteen percent of the parents in the middle income group could not recollect where they had gone for the purpose of vaccination.

In the richer section, it was found that nearly sixty percent of the children were taken to government dispensaries. And fifteen percent gone to private hospital. Similarly, thirteen percent were taken to both the private and government hospitals. So far as getting vaccination from a local private doctor was concerned it was found that nearly six percent had gone to private. Nearly seven percent could not recollect that where had they taken their children for vaccination.

The study also revealed that all sorts of people whether rich or poor (maximum number of children) visited government dispensary followed by clinic and private practitioner for the purpose of vaccination.

The Family Welfare Programme

The Municipal Corporation of Delhi (M.C.D.) dispensaries were primarily entrusted with carrying out the family welfare programme. The lady doctor incharge of the M.C.D. dispensaries were not only to carry out the health care activities of women and children but also to carry out the promotion and propagation of concept of the family welfare amongst the women and their husband.

The O.P.D. of the hospitals or the dispensary were being used by the doctors as well as the other staff for the purpose of family welfare activities i.e. propagation of the massage, social mobilisation, distribution of contraceptives, besides some minor clinical consultancy being given by the doctors to the women. But so far as door to door activities of family welfare was concerned, the Auxiliary Nurse Midwives (A.N.M.) and the Lady Health Visitors (L.H.V.) used to go to the houses, for persuasion of the eligible couples to get sterilised, in each case the A.N.M. or the L.H.V. were getting certain amount of remuneration as incentive.

It was found that for the class four and class three staffs, the programme of family welfare was more of a target oriented time bound battle, where, some staffs of the centre did not mind putting their every thing at stake.

The study also revealed that the oral contraceptives were most of the time not available. And, it is mostly condoms which were available and the house wives visited the centre or dispensary to get the condoms. The only probable reason of more tubectomy can be ascribed to the inhibition of male members for getting sterilised. Moreover, they believed bread winner should remain strong sterilisation will weaken them. Queries were made to know the methods of contraceptives being applied in the community. One women called Shanti was asked about the contraceptives, she said the following words :

> ....once she had gone to the dispensary of Jahangirpuri, for getting copper-T inserted, in order to stop conceptions. the staff told her that they do not plant Copper-T. She should go to the hospital. But she did not have time to go to any one the hospitals, whether to Babu Jagjivan Ram or to Kasturba Gandhi. Moreover, she came to know that insertion of Copper-T was quite painful matter because her neighbour who got the Copper-T. always complained of pain in the back, general weakness and irregular menses. When she had sought her neighbours advice for Copper-T, she told that it is better to opt for oral pills or to use the condoms than insertion of IUD......

Another lady called Laxmi a friend of Shanti said,

> ,.........: the staffs of these dispensaries are so rude in behaviour and so careless that once who has interacted with them will never go there again, she had Copper-T inserted from a private practitioner without the knowledge of her husband and continued with the same although she had

told to her husband about it in due course of time. After one year she had gone to the government dispensary of the locality for its removal, they said they did not plant so they will not remove the IUD. As they did not remove she had to go to private clinic to get the Copper-T removed....

An attempt was made to find out the awareness of the people about the types of contraceptive methods being practised in their community.

The following table shows that amongst the poor the preference of condoms was quite high followed by the operation. So far as operation or sterilisation was concerned it was a kind of a thrusted option on these people or in other words the method of sterilisation was known to all due to, compulsory sterilisation people had to undergo during national emergency in the country. Incentives given for sterilisation in some cases were a piece of land or in some cases cash award and in case of government servant one increament, in the salary or even promotion at times.

As many as forty three percent of the residents could not say whether any contraceptive method was being adopted in their community or not. So far as the poor were concerned they hardly took any kind of oral pills. Ten percent of the poor could not say whether in their colony they had any kind of contraceptives available or had provision of any contraceptive in the dispensaries.

Table: 5.15

Distribution of Practice of Various Methods of Family Welfare in Three Income Groups in the Study Area

Income Group	*Oral Pills*	*Condoms*	*Serialisation*	*Nothing Available*	*Do not Know*
Poor	0	30 (31.57%)	25 (26.31%)	10 (10.52%)	30 (31.57%)
Middle	0	35 (21.0%)	17 (10.24%)	8 (4.81%)	106 (63.85%)
Rich	2 (3.70%)	30 (55.55%)	17 (31.48%)	5 (9.25%)	0
Total	2/315	95/315	59/315	23/315	136/315

In case of middle income group, it was found that no one talked of oral pills. In the same stratum twenty percent said that the method adopted for family welfare was condom. And ten percent only said that family welfare can be had by sterilisation only. A small amount of five percent in the middle section said that nothing was available in the local health care centres, particularly the contraceptives. Almost sixty four percent of the middle income group could not say anything clearly about the practices in the community.

In case of rich, it was found that nearly four percent of the women talked of oral pills for women as contraceptives. In other words, they could also visualise the oral pills as viable method for contraception. And at the same time nearly fifty six percent of the middle income group of the colony and the villagers said that they feel most common method for family welfare was usage of condom. And nearly thirty two percent of the same category of people were of the opinion that the sterilisation was quite common amongst the local resident. Only nine percent said that there was nothing available in the colony.

By and large one can say from the above mentioned table that majority of the people knew about two things very clearly i.e. condom and sterilisation, and those were most common and no group difference was observed regarding the usage of the two popular contraceptive methods. And at the same time, many people said that they did not know what were the types of family welfare measures being adopted.

In the same light, queries were made to the individual households and families to know about the family welfare measures being taken at individual household level.

The study showed that amongst poor, forty two percent of the people were using condom. And about thirty seven percent of the poor had undergone sterilisation. Sixteen percent of the poor people were practising the contraceptive initially and later on accepted sterilisation. Only, five percent of the poor could not tell about their practice and some of them did not want to tell about the method adopted.

Amongst the middle income group of the colony thirty percent of the people were using the contraceptive method i.e. condom. Eighteen percent of the middle class people got sterilised. So far as the contraceptive and the operation was concerned thirty seven percent of them have agreed that they used the methods for family welfare purpose. And only one percent practised Coitus Interruptus (deliberate check from complete intercourse) as method of family planning. Nearly fourteen percent of the middle strata people did not want to tell the methods they practised.

Table: 5.16

Distribution of Practice of Various Methods of Family Welfare in Three Income Groups in the Family

Income Group	*Contra-Ceptive (condom)*	*Sterlisation*	*Contra-Ceptive & Sterilisation*	*Conitus Interruptius (Practice)*	*Can't Say*
Poor	40 (42.10)	35 (36.84)	15 (15.78)	-	5 (5.26)
Middle	40 (30.12)	30 (18.0)	61 (26.74)	2 (1.2)	23 (13.85)
Rich	22 (30.74)	10 (18.51)	13 (24.04)	4 (7.4)	5 (9.25)
Total	112/315	75/315	89/315	6/315	33/315

Among the rich thirty one percent of the population followed contraceptive methods. Nearly eighteen percent of the rich followed method of sterilisation.

A quarter of the rich had practised both the sterilisation and contraceptive methods. So far as Coitus - Interrupts was concerned seven percent of the rich practised it. Nine percent of the rich did not want to say that what was the type of family welfare measure they had adopted or were adopting.

The desire to have at least one male child or to have more number of children in the family were important determinants which ultimately determines the family size. The desire of the family to have more number of children was also found to be very high.

Amongst forty three percent of the poor they said that they were happy with maximum of three children. And fifty three percent were of the opinion that having four to six children are one of the necessities for the poor. The strong arguments given in favour having such large family and number of children are :

— Number of children means number of working hand.

— They are productive unit in the domestic and external fronts.

--- Moreover, the number of children are blessing of God

--- And finally some of them felt that having many children is a good sign.

Table: 5.17

Distribution of Number of Child Desired by Parents in Three Strata

Income Group	*Desired 1 to 3 Children*	*Desired 4 to 6 Children*	*Desired More than 6*	*Not Applicable*
Poor	41 (43.15)	50 (52.63%)	4 (4.2)	-
Middle	70 (42.16)	68 (40.96%)	3 (12.0)	8 (4.8)
Rich	40 (74.0)	6 (11.11)	3 (5.55)	5 (9.25)
Total	151/315	124/315	27/315	13/315

And almost four percent of the poor said that they have even more than six children.

In case of middle class, forty two percent desired only, one to three children. Forty one percent of the people in this community endorsed that they had four to six children and it was quite normal to have those many children. Twelve percent of the households in this group were desirous to have more than six children, but all of them also agreed that the basic reason for such size was the result of unfulfilled dream to have at least two sons in a family. Whereas, five percent of the middle class did not have any children. In case of seventy four percent rich households, were contented with one to three children at the most, and they were not too eager to have son at the cost of large family size. Eleven percent of the richer section of the population had more than four but less than six children, they also justified their craving for such family size by arguing to have sons. And five percent had more than six children and the reason given by these families for such size was to have son was primarily for the security of the future and for managing their family business in future and also to advance their family a son is a must.

The study also revealed that nine percent of the richer section were having no children and neither they showed any kind of inclination to have any child. Contray, it was observed that not a single poor family was issueless, whereas there were more than fifty percent of the households who had more than four and less than six children. Desire to have male child was universal. In other words, religion and caste did not change the common desire to have a male child. And it was also found from the study that the Muslims of the colony insisted for more children or in other words the norm of small family was a far cry in their community. For the Muslims, the number of issues were the prerogative of the Allaha, the supreme God.

During interrogation about the number of children and the various methods being adopted for family welfare by the the Muslims, one Bengali Muslim of block-C, Mr. Khalil presented the facts in the following words,

> .....In "Shariat", Allaha has never asked or given permission to do any thing by which they can stop a child who is destined to come on this earth. And things like use of condom, sterilisation are great sins, no Muslim can get sterilised, if, some one gets sterilised then he becomes "Kaffir", (a man who is against Islam) he cannot remain a Pak (holy) Muslim", and he is bound to get Bahist (hell) after his death. And no body wants Bahist, everybody wants "Janhat" (heaven)..... on the contrary the Kuran gives permission of four Nikaha (marriages) and at the same time all the four wives should bear child for the successful consummation of marriage. So, a child born in a family is an Ammanat (asset) of Allaha. So, nobody has right to check any child. And Allaha is great and he only will give to eat.....

This type of feeling was very common amongst most of the Muslim residents of that area. Moreover sterlisation means the individual will bleed. Bleeding for sterlisation will be crime against Islam. One will pay price for such crime.

As malaria is one of the highly prevalent disease causing high morbidity and at times mortality as well, it was essential to know the status of the disease in the colony and the village. The disease of malaria was studied in the colony and the village amongst the various income groups of the area and the impact of the same on their health status was also observed.

Malaria and Its Status in the Community

In order to know about the status of malaria in the colony of Jahangirpuri and the village Bhalasawa, the perception of the disease, antidotes taken for checking the disease of malaria have been studied in depth. Types of cure and the organisation where cure was sought were equally important parameter, so those parameters were also found out.

From the following table it become clear that almost seventy four percent or two third of the poor people said that malaria means shivering fever with high body temperature. Nine percent of the poor household said that it was always with shooting fever. Only two percent said it was associated with vomiting. Ten percent said that malaria means fever, body and head ache along with vomiting. Remaining four percent of poor people could not recollect any symptoms of malaria.

Table: 5.18

Distribution of Symptoms Perceived for Malaria by Three Strata

Income Group	Chilling Fever with Shiver	Shooting Fever	Vomiting	Fever, ache Vomiting	Can't Say
Poor	70 (73.7%)	9 (9.47%)	2 (2.1%)	10 (10.52%)	4 (4.2%)
Middle	104 (62.6%)	12 (7.22%)	5 (3.0%)	35 (21.68%)	9 (5.4%)
Rich	40 (74.07%)	5 (9.25%)	1 (1.85%)	8 (14.81%)	-
Total	214/315	26/315	8/315	54/315	13/315

Among the middle section sixty two percent of the resettlers and villagers defined malaria as fever with shiver and high body temperature. Seven percent said that it causes shooting fever. Three percent said it was combined with vomiting. Nearly twenty two percent were of the opinion that it was combined with body ache, fever and vomiting. Five percent could not say about the symptoms of malaria.

In case of the rich people, seventy four percent of the respondents said malaria means chilling sensation combined with shivering fever. Only nine percent of the people said it mainfested in the form of shooting fever. Roughly, two percent said that in case of malaria the patient vomits. Nearly fifteen percent of the people of rich community were of the opinion that malaria has to have fever, body and headache as well as vomiting.

It was realised from the study that irrespective of different economic strata majority of the people perceived malaria as fever with shiver and rise of body temperature. And to a large extent people of the three different strata said that it is combination of body and headache as well as vomiting (when a person suffers from malaria). Another prominent observation made during study was a small section of poor and the middle strata did not know any kind of signs or symptoms of malaria whereas, amongst the richer section of the population every one knew signs and symptoms of malaria.

Why is the prevalence of malaria so high in the resettlement colony, was asked to a man called Ram Bahadur, who explained about the reasons of such high prevalence.

> .....the spread of malaria in the colony is nothing surprising, the gutters are open and filthy, drains are over flowing and not a single MCD sweeper, comes or cleans the place inspite of their assignment. No body sprayed oil on the surface of the gutters. Moreover, all open spaces in the colony got converted into garbage dumping ground and everything is dumped there by the residents of the colony and by the villagers as well. So sooner it rains the whole area gets filled with water and mosquitoes breed and no staff of municipality comes to clean it. Contrary people dig out soil from such empty spaces which subsequently becomes dug outs filled with water and filth. And no municipality worker comes to fill up the dug-outs or to kill the eggs or larvae of mosquitoes inspite of repeated complains....

In order to have more broader perspective of malaria menace of the locality, a resident of the village Bhalasawa was asked, regarding malaria prevalence. Mr. Lekh Pal of village Bhalasawa said,

> .....it is next to impossible to sit within the house or out side after 6 p.m. in the village. The village is situated at a very low plane and surrounded by ditches and dug-outs which are full of dirty water. The situation is getting aggravated day by day as areas surrounding the village are getting filled with the filth of the resettlement.....

On enquiring about the resettlers role for the aggravation of the situation. Mr. Lekh Pal replied in the following words,

> ...."Delhi Development Authority has installed a pump for suction of waste water right behind the block-E, there is a booster motor besides suction pump inside a room which is controlled and regulated by a government employee. All those filth which are sucked are thrown across

> the by-pass-dam. As the area across the dam is too low lying. it act as good reservoir for the dirty water and the lowlying area is connected with the village, water gets logged around the village. The logged water has no outlet as a result it stagnate and became a breeding ground for mosquitoes. It is our misfortune that every time M.P. or any other official of the area comes here always reassures that something will be done to solve the problem. but when they go back they do not do any thing for this problem"....

Another villager, Mr. Shankar Lal had to say the following words regarding the water loging at the entrance of the village,

> ..dug-outs were initially not there but as more and more illegal constructions of houses were coming up on the front side of the village, digging of soil from this part became a common feature. Moreover, earlier this dug out was being used for bathing few buffalos of the village, now all the cattles of the village are brought here for bathing, inspite of knowing the disadvantage of such logging no body cares rather they try to ignore the problem and close their eyes towards the problem...

"Regarding malaria worker".... Mr. Shankar Lal said,

> ".....The malaria workers of the area are seen once in five or six months time, some times they come with the oil to be sprayed in those dig-outs. some times they come without any kind of oil, but simply scribble on the wall, so that, any higher official who comes for investigation. always gets an impression that the workers are regularly coming in the village. So far as chloroquin distribution is concerned. if there is a patient of malaria in the village then only they distribute the medicine. But if any body ask for it, most of the time they say it is out of stock"......

For the malaria cases of the village and the resettlement colony, patients were supposed to be taken to MCD dispensary and from there the blood smear be given to the technicians of the J-block's MCD run dispensary. One of the respondents from Block-I Mr. Shekh Mohmed, was asked how are they treated when doctor suspect that they are suffering of malaria. He narrated his experience in the following words.

> he was suffering of intermittent shooting fever, initially he had taken all the available medicines for fever at home but nothing happened then he went to the doctor in the dispensary. The doctor on listening the whole case gave him some tablets and also asked him to visit the dispensary

early morning around 8 a.m. So, he followed doctor's advise and reached there very next day. A man had asked him to give some blood drops for testing, although it is against Quran to give blood but he had given some blood for testing purpose. As per the instruction he went to the same dispensary after three days to collect his report they told him report is perfectly alright, he got convinced. And by God's grace he was having no fever for four days but on the very fifth day fever relapsed, and he could not go to work and kept lying on bed. This time he went to a private doctor for the purpose of treatment. As he narrated the whole case to the doctor, he gave him same tablets once again took some smear and asked him to take the report on the next morning. As he went there the very next morning he was told that it is a clear case of malaria. And the doctor also gave him the full course of medicine besides, certain dos and don'ts. Although, he had to spend money but he got definite relief from the problem of repeated shooting fever.....

The above mentioned case clearly showed that the government run dispensaries were less accountable and careful about the test and diagnosis, whereas the private doctor was serious about his job. Even, though he charged but gave definite cure to the patient. The study also showed that a poor patient would go to private practitioner and pay to get cured because in government dispensaries he would have to go again and again but even then he might not get cured and at the same time he would keep loosing his wage due to absenteeism. One more factor also became clear that the technicians were both negligent and incompetent and they could afford to remain so, as they knew there would not be any kind of disciplinary action against them. And so far the supply of medicine was concerned it was also erratic in nature, as the supply of medicine was purely the domain of National Malaria Eradication Programme (NMEP) presently called as *National Anti Malaria Programme* (NAMP). They could get away by simply saying that the "medicine is out of stock".

Some glaring problems were found out easily in the locality. In other words, there were certain diseases or ailments which could be found in high prevalence in the colony of Jahangirpuri as well as in the village. In some areas, the disease had taken the magnitude of endemicity. One of the most common diseases in the area was gastro-enteritis. The problem of gastro-enteritis and allied diseases were spreading primarily due to the polluted water supply system. Improper storing of water used for drinking. Besides, the cut fruits which were sold cheaply and were consumed by almost all the poor people of the colony and the village, particularly during the summer months contamination and infection of the cut foods used to be very high.

Mostly the children became victim of such diseases as the drinking water as well as foods taken outside their home were mostly infested with lots of germs. It was observed that as the ailment of gastro-enteritis was quite common in this area all the private practitioners and even the government dispensaries did always keep the required medicine in stock. And for the general practitioners of the colony the problem of gastro-enteritis was the largest profit earner or in other words the maximum share of their practice was by curing the patient of GI ailments.

In the study, an attempt was made to know that where do they take their child when the child suffer of gastro-entritis. And it was also found out that which income group fell easy pray to gastro-entritis and what remedial measure they take to prevent the disease.

Table: 5.19

Treatment Availed from Different Type of Health Institution by the Gastro-entritis Patients of Three Strata

Income Group	*To Allopathic Doctor*	*To local quack*	*Home remedy*	*Naturopathy*
Poor	65 (68.42%)	15 (15.78%)	10 (10.52%)	5 (5.26%)
Middle	86 (51.80%)	29 (17.46%)	40 (24.09%)	11 (6.62%)
Rich	54 (100%)	-	-	-
Total	205/315	44/315	50/315	16/315

It can be seen from the table 5.19 that majority of the poor children of the colony and the village had been taken to allopathic doctor (almost seventy percent of the people went to allopathic doctor). Sixteen percent of the poor went to the quacks for the cure of gastro-entritis. Ten percent of the poor relied exclusively on home remedy. Almost five percent of the patients relied absolutely on the natural therapy, who did not consult any doctor or quack they let the ailment get cured in its natural course.

On the issue of local remedy the for gastro-entritis, Mrs. Munni Bai of Block-K said that,

> She had been visiting Mr. Banwarilal for last ten years since the inception of the colony. As her five year old child was suffering of stomach trouble, he was vomiting, going to latrine again and again. So she had taken the son to him. He touched the pulse of the son and thereafter asked him to lie on the floor. As the son lied down he gave gentle massage to him. Then he was asked to get up and Mr. Banwarilal did some water sponging. And, finally he made him gulp a solution which was made by him only. Moreover, he gave her some black powder and asked to make solution of the same in a glass full of water. She was curious to known the substance used in the powder but, he was not ready to tell but after repeated requests he told her that it is nothing but a particular concentration of opium and water. And she found that after three days the son who was not in a position to get up from bed was ready to play and move around with friends. Besides, he did not complain of any kind of side effect. So, she though that she must consult with him for any kind of disease or ailment in future.....

For the home remedy of children's gastro-entritis, one villager called Sunder Lal, told the following,

> when the child suffer of gastro-entritis or of similar ailment, he gives home remedy which is primarily based on the type foods which the suffering child refuses. He was absoltely confident that food is the only solution for the cure of gastric diseases. When a child suffers of gastro-entritis he is given certain specific diet i.e. curd and rice, but not any spicy curry, no oily or greasy food is given to the child. In many cases, where the child is suffering of loose motion he is given green banana curry as an antidote of the problem. If, such diet is continued for two to three days child gets cured. In some cases, kedegree is given as a replacement to general routine diet (cooked pulse and rice with little salt and turmeric)....

The food taboos for the gastro-entritis adopted by the people instead of visiting to the allopathic or homeopathic dispensaries or to the quacks were more common in this area.

Most of the ladies of the colony as well as the village said the treatment for GI trouble in the following wards. They give an ayurvedic medicine known as *Amritanjan*, they also give a mixture of lemon water with salt or sugar, some allopathic medicine along with other medicines. In some cases, when the child complained of nausea but not able to vomit a particular dilution of saline water was given for stomach wash....

The above description shows that in many of the cases where allopathic medicine was not taken as such, there the patient was given a definite proportion or mix of allopathic medicine with the local therapy in the form of food taboos or conventional local concoctions. But, the patients were mostly taken to allopathic doctor and even if the older generation knows about the cure they were either not encouraged or they were not interested of their own to practice local or home remedies.

The above table also showed that in case of middle class, nearly fifty eight percent of the children were taken to the allopathic doctor. Whereas, seventeen percent of the children had been taken to the local quacks. And a quarter of the children in the middle class were given home remedy. It was also found that more than six percent of the children did not take any kind of remedy.

In case of children of this group it was found that cent percent of the children had been taken to the allopathic doctor and they had been given allopathic medicine only. The most probable reasons for this kind of visiting patterns been explained as:

- The allopathic medicine is more scientific, so it is always better.
- The rich section could afford to pay and the allopathic doctor charged more, so they visited there.

In order to know what sort of weaning diet is given or to whom the child is taken for consultation besides, what do the parents do when a child of pre-school or of school age group suffers of gastro-entritis, mainly with severe cases of diahorrea and dysentery certain queries were raised. As this was the most common disease it was also essential to know the spread of this disease as well as the causative factors or pathogenesis and the type of remedial measures taken to prevent the menance of such kind of disease. The diseases was so common as a result it had direct bearing on the health of the people particularly the children.

An attempt was made to know the details of treatment methods adopted by the people when their children suffered of diahorrea or dysentery.

It became clear from the above table that majority of the people were going to the allopathic practitioner irrespective of their economic status. Amongst the poor seventy nine percent of the children were taken to the allopathic doctor. Ten percent of the poor had controlled food in order to control the diahorrea and dysentery. Five percent of the poor had been doing self medication for their children's problems.

Table: 5.20

Consultancy Patterns of Various Strata of Children in Case of Diahorrea & Dysentery

Income Group	*Doctors Advise*	*Food Control*	*Self Medication*	*Can't Say*
Poor	75	10	5	5
	(78.94)	(10.52)	(5.26%)	(5.26)
Middle	147	8	5	6
	(88.55)	(4.81)	(3.01%)	(3.61)
Rich	50	3	1	
	(92.59)	(5.55%)	(1.85%)	(0)
Total	272/315	21/315	11/315	11/315

Around five percent of the poor could not say clearly that what did they do, when any of their child suffered of gastro-entritis.

In case of middle class, it was found that as large as eighty eight percent of the people had taken their children to allopathic doctors. Whereas, only five percent relied on food control remedy. So far as self medication was concerned a little more than three percent practised it. And almost equal percentage could not say that what did they do when their child suffered of diahorrea or dysentery.

The study showed that almost ninety three percent of the rich went to doctor during stomach trouble and five percent of the children were under diet control. And two percent did self medication.

Table 5.20 showed some more facts as self medication was done by four percent of the parents irrespective of their economic group. Diet control or food taboo during the ailment of the children was also observed amongst different economic groups but, it was more common amongst the poor.

As cholera is also a dreadful disease for the young and old it also warrants sufficient importance. The children are the first and the foremost victim of this disease and it takes endemic form within twenty four hours of its first out bursts. The scholar went twice to see specifically whether the disease existed there or not. First survey was done during the main study and the second was conducted at a later stage after the out burst of cholera empidemic in the trans-Yamuna resettlement colonies, as a pro-active step.

In the second phase of the study all the households were visited and information was also collected from MCD staff regarding cholera.

The MCD and Delhi Administration staffs were asked regarding the situation of cholera in the colony and in the village. The staffs replied with full authenticity that so far as the resettlement colony was concerned, not a single case been found, whereas for the village they did not do anything. The interrogation was highly essential because at that point of time the prevalence of cholera was at peak in trans-Yamuna resettlement colonies, as the visit of relatives is a common feature between Nand Nagari (a trans-Yamuna colony) and Jahangirpuri.

To understand the clinical and the sub-clinical manifestation of the disease, the doctors were asked about the situation and they told that the disease did not take serious turn in Jahangirpuri as it was in case of trans-Yamuna area due to certain preventive measures. But, at the same time, they admitted that thier report was based on the provisional diagnosis of the patients. So, one or two cases might have been there because the conditions of the resettlement colonies were not too much different from each other. Moreover, it did not attain any alarming status as it had in the resettlement colonies of trans-Yamuna. In due course of conversation with the doctors, they admitted that they did not have any pathological testing facility for cholera bacteria. In case of any suspicion through signs and symptoms of the patients, the patients were either referred to the Infectious Disease Hospital, or in some cases the samples were sent to the general hospital for testing, in such circumstance the hospital used to send back the report in two days or some times in three days time. This delay could cause spread of the disease in the community extensively, but by gods grace everything was under control.

So, it was clear from the above statement that the spread of such a diseases were possible and the doctor would have been helpless in case of an epidemic. Moreover, the amount of medicines they had in stock was not sufficient in case of any outburst.

It was clear from the study that almost every kind of diseases or health problem were existing in that area, and those could be categorised broadly into few groups, minor ailment, major ailment, chronic ailment, accident etc. Besides, there were various kinds of communicable diseases which were equally common in this area. It was revealed from the study that problem of mother and child was of equally high concern as that of any other diseases in the area.

One of the most common diseases in that area was Tuberculosis. This disease had attained very serious magnitude in the colony and the village.

Tuberculosis : An Overview

During the study, a detailed inquiry regarding the spread prevalence, care, cure and the follow-up measure of tuberculosis (T.B.) patients were made in the community. It was also important to know about T.B. and its various manifestations, as the people of the area were poor so they were prone to it. It was also necessary to know what do they do in case of T.B. As it was well-known fact that the disease of T.B. is curable provided the full course of medication is carried out. Sufficient idea was gathered regarding people's awareness of the disease of T.B. In order to know the people's perception or level of awareness regarding T.B. the members of the households of Jahangirpuri and the village were asked about the signs and symptoms of T.B. in great detail.

Table 5.21 shows that around fifty three percent of the poor said chronic cough and weakness as the main symptom of the disease. Twelve percent of the poor said T.B. meant weakness and fever. Six percent of the poor said that T.B. manifests with paleness and chest pain. Nearly sixteen percent of the poor thaught that blood in cough as one of the most common feature of the disease. Eight percent of the poor said breathlessness as one of the most common feature of T.B. They feel breathlessness was more amongst the poor because they were mostly engaged in hard and manual works combined with malnutrition. And nearly five percent of the poor could not tell what were the signs and symptoms of T.B.

In case of middle class forty two percent of the people said that it was associated with chronic cough and weakness. Nine percent said that T.B. also connotes weakness and fever. Where as six percent of the middle class said that T.B. meant paleness and chest pain. Nearly eight percent said that it was indicated by the blood in the cough of the patient. Six percent of the middle income group said that T.B. meant breathlessness. And twenty eight percent said that they have heard of T.B. but did not know sign and symptoms of the disease.

Table - 5.21

Pattern of Perception of TB in Different Income Strata

Income Group	*Chronic Cough & Weakness*	*Weakness & Fever*	*Paleness & Chest*	*Blood in Cough*	*Breathing Trouble*	*Can't Say*
Poor	50 (52.63)	11 (11.57)	6 (6.31)	15 (15.7)	8 (8.42)	5 (5.2)
Middle	70 (42.16)	15 (9.03)	11 (6.62)	13 (7.8)	10 (6.0)	47 (28%)
Rich	38 (70.37)	5 (9.25)	9 (16.66)	2 (3.7)		

Seventy percent of the rich said that chronic cough and weakness symbolised tuberculosis. At the same time, nine percent said that T.B. patient suffers of weakness and fever. Almost seventeen percent of the rich identified T.B. with paleness and chest pain. And four percent of the rich were of the opinion that in case of tuberculosis the patient gets blood in sputum.

Table 5.21 showed clearly that T.B. had been perceived and understood in various ways by the various strata of people. But one factor was very clear from the data that fifty percent of the respondents irrespective of their economic class equivocally said that T.B. was mainly weakness and chronic cough. Although, rest of the symptoms were also reported as manifestation of T.B. with lesser stress. It was observed, the disease proved fatal in case of mal-treatment also in case of defaulters of any type, (not taking regular treatment due to irregular drug supply or carelessness of health care institutions).

Looking into the magnitude of the disease spread it became essential to go into larger details of the disease manifestation, cure and care besides the status of the follow-up cases of T.B. and their status after cure was also enquired during the study from the people of the area.

Babu Lal, a 42 year old sweeper of Municipal Corporation of Delhi (MCD), a resident of block-C, on asking about T.B. told the following words;

> He was having cough and used to feel cold and at times, his body used to have high temperature combined with headache, as he reported of these symptoms to doctor of the local dispensary, doctor gave cough syrup and

tablets to control fever and headache. He was reluctant to consult any other doctor inspite of his repeated problem, whenever he complained of more pain and ache he was prescribed strong medicine which he used to purchase from the market but the relief of those medicines did not last long.

One fine morning he was totally unable to go for his duty due to chest pain. He started vomiting blood and after sometimes he fell unconscious. He did not know what happened there after but when he regained consciousness he found himself in hospital. He was taken to Babu Jagjivan Ram Memorial Hospital in the colony. Although, he could not stay there as it is a general hospital so, he was referred to Rajan Babu T. B. Hospital (RBTB). He stayed there for full one month and in those days at least one junior doctor used to visit him every day at his bed site. One senior doctor used to do the checking once a week. He was a chain smoker earlier but as long as he remained admitted he did not smoke at all. Although, some times he used to smoke in bathroom or latrine after hoodwinking the doctors and nurses. However, on release he was having no cough cold or weakness but he was weak enough to do any arduous work. During his release the doctor advised for many do's and don'ts for eating and drinking besides, his limit to do physical work was fixed, the amount and type of food to be taken was also determined by the doctor. But he could not give up smoking at home nor could he keep up with the food taboos or special diet recommended to him. The habits are too old to die and the special diet was not possible due to the financial constrains, so he was taking his regular food only.

He was asked to visit by the doctors at least once a month but he did not go for the follow-up, as in this case he would loose his salary and many other facilities. As a result of which he tried to purchase those tablets from the market but he could succeed once or twice only, afterward he had to stop personal purchase as it was too dear to his pocket. He had full prescription of treatment and the medicine with that he approached to E-block dispensary and showed the papers to the doctors there and they agreed to give him the medicine and he was given the medicine for three months regularly in the E-block dispensary. But there after nothing was given to him. To go to hospital and get medicine in OPD in RBTB hospital was even more harder as he could not stand in queue for such long period to get medicine so his treatment remained incomplete and he continued to suffer.

It becomes clear from the above case that the things were not yet up to the mark. The sufferers are yet many and they are not cared for at the initial stage by the health care authorities. Only such cases were treated locally, those who were treated by the RBTB hospital initially Follow-up of treatment mostly remained hampered as the poor patient either could not afford to go to the local dispensary or to the OPD of the hospital, going to fetch medicine every week at the cost of their job was a hard task for them. Endless queues of the hospital or the dispensary aggravated the situation of the patient care to a large extent.

Such situations demand quick and effective method of diagnosis of cases, immediate treatment and medical consultancy besides, a systematic and simple technique of follow-up. It was observed that as the patient used to get temporary relief when treated in the hospital, but the day when he was discharged he became reluctant in many ways and became defaulter. And within no time the cas relapsed and the patient once again became an active case of T.B. which needed far more rigorous and regular treatment, otherwise such neglect lead to grave consequences.

In order to know the reaction of the relatives or the friends of the T.B. patients towards the disease and its magnitude, questions were asked to the elderly of the households. It was essential in the light of the general perception to know whether it was a dreaded disease (as per their perception) and if any one had contacted it then should he or she be secluded or not, or if the family could afford his or her treatment. Given such backdrop, issues were raised to the people of the area.

Table: 5.22

Step Adopted in Case of TB by Three Different Strata of People of Jahangirpuri & Bhalaswa

Income Group	*Seclusion & Avoidance*	*Treatment to be Given*	*Doctors Advice*	*Can't Say*
Poor	72	12	4	7
	(75.78)	(12.6)	(4.21)	(7.3)
Middle	115	08	3	40
	(69.27)	(4.81)	(1.80)	(24.0)
Rich	40	6	2	6
	(74.07)	(11.11)	(3.70)	(11.11)
Total	227/315	26/315	9/315	53/315

Amongst the poorer section, it was found that nearly seventy six percent of the people said that policy of seclusion and avoidance was the best. Nearly thirteen percent of the poor said that treatment should be given to the T.B. patient. And seven percent of them said that they cannot say that what should be done with the T.B. patients.

In case of middle income section, it was found that sixty nine percent of them were of the opinion that the patients should be secluded and avoided. Around five percent of the people said that treatment should be given to the patients. Nearly two percent of the middle income people said that doctors advise and good food should be given to T.B. patients. Whereas a quarter of the middle income people were unable to tell what type of treatment should be given.

Amongst the rich seventy four percent said the patient should be secluded and avoided. Eleven percent of the rich people said that treatment should be given to T.B. patient. Four percent of the rich said that T.B. patient should be given doctors advice and good food. And eleven percent of the rich people could not say what should be done for the T.B. patient.

Table 5.22 showed that majority (72%) have agreed that seclusion and avoidance of T.B. patient was one of the most acceptable way. It was known to the people of the area that it is a contagious disease, so people were a bit sceptical to carry out domiciliary treatment as well as the follow-up treatment of T.B. cases at home. In this connection respondent from Block-C, Mr. Duli Chand said,

> His wife was a T.B. case and his children were small, they were not in a position to stay away from their mother. He had been trying to keep the children away but was not successful. Moreover, house was so small that all of them lived in very close proximity to each other and each one of them were highly vulnerable but more so were the children. Wife was a open case of T.B. She could be admitted to RBTB hospital but if she were to be admitted then he had no one to look after the children at home. Whereas, he knew he could not give her the treatment of the hospital at home, although he was trying to get her medicines which he had been told by the specialist for T.B. He was thinking to bring one of his distant relative from Bihar but that would take time. For the time being, he was taking medicine from the E-block dispensary. Later on, he took her to RBTB for admission. As a result of his wife's ailment he was suffering physically (suffering of intermittent cough and weakness) and mentally as well.

The above narration clearly shows that even if the domicilliary treatment of T.B. was an accepted and established fact but it could not be practised due to various limitations to implement (in case of the poor people) as per doctors instruction.

To find out the meaning and perception of major disease it was essential to carry out the study amongst the colony and village people. The study helped to understand the people's perception and behaviour towards the disease like Tuberculosis. Various kinds of accidents among the three starta of the population also was a part of the study. In case of minor ailment, it was observed that the people did not visit to the doctor or dispensary most of the time. They generally took medicine which they knew and were given earlier for same problem, using of left over medecine or purchasing the same medicine without consulting doctor was a common practice to treat the minor ailment at their own level. Besides, they did not take bath if they were having cough and cold. If it is headache then they applied one or the other balm. In case of cuts or bruise they applied Boroline, Burnol or similar type of antiseptic creams.

The major ailments (communicable and non-communicable) were important to be studied as such studies will give opportunities to understand the affect and interaction of the disease, patient and organisational behaviour towards the various level of patients by the doctors, nurses and paramedics. Moreover, in such situations how did the entire family of the patient behave. The socio-economic life style of the patients family is affected by the magnitude of ailment and suffering, besides, rate of cure of the patients within and subsequently without hospital. Keeping such things in mind it was necessary to study the major diseases.

Major Non-communicable Diseases

The study revealed different types of patients suffering of various types of major diseases. One such case could be cited in the present study. Mr. Ramesh Kumar an employee of Indian Airlines father of an unfortunate child called Gooddi told how the child suffered and still in a bad shape due to the mis-diagnosis and carelessness of the doctors, of the local private practitioner and of the doctors of various governmental organisations, emotionally charged Ramesh Kumar told the whole episode in a chronological manner in the following words:

His only daughter Goddi who was sick for last three years and she was bed-ridden for twenty four hours a day so he needed some person to look after his daughter. It all started three years ago when all of a sudden she fell ill as she was having high temperature. Such state of hyperpyrexia continued for seven days at a stretch. She refused to take any kind of medicine as well as food but somehow his wife and himself were able to force some food and medicines down her throat.

She became quite alright after seven days of suffering. But she became very weak and pale, considering her condition he took the daughter to the panel doctor of India Airlines. This panel of doctor gave medicine worth Rs. 500/-. But she did not recover fully even after taking costly medicines. She once again fell ill after one month showing old signs and symptoms. Thereafter, she was taken to Hindu Rao. She was admitted in the hospital without much fuss. She was kept in the general wards initially for few days but later she was shifted to in Intensive Care Unit (ICU). She was being checked by various doctors but no body could tell exact disease of his daughter, whereas in the mean time he had spent Rs. 5000/- on the purchase of costly medicines. Moreover, he knew that all that expenditure which he was incurring would be reimbursed by the Indian Airlines. (Ramesh Kumar's employer).

But the saddest part of all was that when his child was discharged after one month she was suffering of paralyse of limb and face. And the facial paralysis had affected her speech as well.

A senior doctor of the hospital told him that it is a case of brain cancer. The pronouncement of the doctor not only made them extremely sorry but also disheartend. By that time she became so much handicapped that it became necessary to have one round the clock attendant for her. To meet the needs and demands of the child there were no body who could come forward and help. His son was even much more younger than his daughter. As a result his wife had to resign from the school teachership, and started looking after the daughter.

He could not bear with such traumatic situation so, he could not sit idle. He took his daughter to the Ram Manohar Lohia hospital. Looking into such pathetic situation and going through the earlier case history, they gave her admission but that admission was more of an experiment on his daughter rather than treatment. He used to watch those things mutely as he knew doctors also have no other go than to go by trial and error method, within few days time she was shifted to ICU from the general ward. All sorts of experiments proved futile in Ram Manohar Lohia. They discharged her after one month trail but suggested to take the child to Govind Ballabh Panth Hospital. On asking them what did they suspect, they replied that they suspected viral infection of brain. By that time his daughter not only became paralytic and speech less but also started having impaired vision.

But in due course of treatments in Ram Manohar Lohia, he had already spend Rs. 10000/-. He had taken the daughter to Govind Ballabh Panth hospital as per the advise of the doctors to get C.T. scan done as the facility of scanning was available in Govind Ballabh Panth. It was not difficult for his daughter to get admission there as she was referred from RML hospital. After her admission she was taken care by a neuro-surgeon, he was also of the opinion that first step would be scanning. Doctor referred for scanning and he took the daughter for scanning. Ramesh Kumar was told to wait for the scan result. Looking into the urgency of the case, he was suggested to get the scanning done privately. He took the child to one of the private scanner, got the seanning done by paying Rs. 1500/-. He was handed over the report immediately the same was taken to the doctor. After going through the scan report the doctor told that the daughter needs brain surgery. He was asked for consent for the operation. Because, the girl seemed to be suffering of brain T.B. The consent was given to the doctor for the operation. The very next day operation was conducted on her. She was kept for three weeks in the hospital after the operation for recuperation. After the operation within seven days time the daughter got her visions back. She regained her faculty of speech after the operation but the paralytic status of the daughter did not change.

In order to get the daughter cured absolutely he took the daughter to All India Institute of Medical Sciences (AIIMS). She was taken to OPD. she attended regularly at the OPD for four to five days. After the parents expressed problem to visit to AIIMS every day from Jahangirpuri, they gave a bed to treat her there as indoor patient. She once again stayed there in the hospital for full one month and in that stay Ramesh Kumar had once again spent around eight thousands rupees.

But he realised that she was not likely to get cured inspite of one month's stay and doctors weren't in a position to tell when she would be cured. Although, they were dutifully carrying out the tests on his daughter. She had little improvement but they got vexed with regular visit to hospital and decided to put her back to home.

But, she remained bed-ridden and needs constant assistance. In this whole process his wife lost her job, the son failed in his class test due to lack of

> study at home as no body could teach him and all of them lost health and both of them became irritable couples.
>
> In the whole course of three years, he had to spend nearly thirty thousand rupees whereas according to him the daughter was leading a vegetable life. He thinks those quacks or "babas" are even better than those who have big degrees from India and abroad. He was fully against purchasing of various gadgets in hospitals by investing so much money as those investment can not cure critical patients like his daughter. And he also feels so many doctors are also not required for our hospital as they can not cure patients. He was fed up with his own daughter at time he thinks that either God should cure her absolutely or take her life........

The above case showed clearly that the patient's father inspite of being rich enough to carry out every test and consultancy as well as check-ups as per the directives of the doctors could not get his daughter cured. The doctors of repute could not come to any specific conclusion for quite some times resulting into spoiling of the case. The doctors did not feel for the case being spoiled by them. It also implies that had the child been from a poor family she would have died long back but as the father of the child and the other family members cooperated she did not die but leading a vegetable life. And, it becomes quite clear that the sate of the art Indian medical and health care system is to a large extent is incapable and unaccountable to the people and patient. The patients as well as her family members worries and anxieties increased so much that after availing the entire range of sophisticated health services in Delhi, they ultimately resorted to the supernatural cure or in other words left the things to gods mercy.

Similarly, one more case of major ailment was reported from the village of Bhalasawa. Mr. Mangoo Singh a farmer, during the interview he was asked whether any body in his house was suffering or not. Mangoo Singh the farmer responded in affirmative. The respondent was reluctant to tell each and every detail as it was clear from his expressions that it is meaningless to repeat the things again and again, so long no body could cure or give any right solution for his son. However, he told the incidence in the following words after a great deal of persuation:

> Mohan his only son born after four daughters, his birth brought umpteen pleasure to him and his wife and elderly of the house. It was all going fine and smooth till he was of four years of age. One evening he was playing

with other children of the village. While playing he fell and broke his leg. He was immediately taken to Hindu Rao hospital as it was emergency case they did not do much fuss to give admission to his son, from emergency he was taken to orthopedics ward and he was kept under the charge of orthopedician and paediatrician. The son was given plaster on his leg and remained admitted for seven days in that hospital.

The son was released from the hospital on the eighth day. The doctor had given a fortnights time for removal of the plaster so he was taken to the hospital on the sixteenth day. But unfortunately on those days all staffs including nurses were on strike. On enquiring from doctors about the probable clouser of strike, one of the staff told him to report after two days, for the removal of the plaster. He took back the son and could not go to hospital for the removal of the plaster after two days, as a result it took another ten days for the removal of the plaster. No sooner the plaster was removed it was realised that the fixing of the bones were improper. Although, the son did not complain of any pain or trouble. The son was taken to the doctor, who had advised for plaster.

After watching the doctor adivised the child for physiotherapy. The needful was done. He started walking of his own after few months but clear change in his gait could be seen. He was advised to rub a kind of oil on his leg and the oil was provided by the hospital, so he kept on rubbing the same but the gait of the son did not change. After some time the son complained about pain in leg. Once again he was taken to another specialist for his problem. After doing thorough scrutiny he told that the bone setting has been done improperly. He also told that nothing has gone wrong he could be once again operate upon, so as to amend the gait Although, initially, Mangoo Singh did not agree but later he agreed to the suggestion. The son was taken to St. Stephens as the doctor had opined for operation at St. Stephens. He showed the paper to the OPD doctors on the day of orthopedics OPD. The doctors of the OPD referred for admission. He was given a card for admission and got the son admitted. A separate room was taken for the son for which Rs. 150/- per day was paid. And he was operated as per schedule. He was discharged after ten days time and was asked to come back to the hospital after seven days. He took his son after seven days to the hospital, his plaster was removed. And after that he was taken there regularly for seven days for getting physiotherapy done. But by the time, the son had developed a deep fear psychosis about the hospital, the doctors as well as nurses. But as luck

> would have it, just after a period of six months he developed a kind of inflammation on the same leg where he was operated upon. And within few months time the problem became serious. He had no other way but to take him once again to hospital and was taken to OPD of Hindu Rao. When it did not work out well he took him to St. Stephen and there after to AIIMS as well.

Inspite of all the running around and regular expenditure on medicines and doctors, the son could not be cured.

> One of the senior orthopedics surgeon of AIIMS told him it was a case of Osteo-myelitis. If the leg had to be saved then he has to be given a full course of costly medicines for one year. To bear such expenses was difficult for Mangoo. Mangoo thinks the son has done a great sin in last birth so he is suffering now and resigned to his faith"........

The above incidence showed quite clearly that even in cases of major and serious ailments the doctors in the locality as well as the hospital were too casual in their approach and which ultimately lead to wrong diagnosis but the doctors did not feel sorry about it, even if the situation worsened. For the mistake of the doctor the patient had to pay quite heavily in terms of time money as well as the quality of life gets spoiled. And at times the life of the nearest and the dearest one get sacrified. In case of the major non communicable diseases, the patient is taken to some quack and simply left at the mercy of god because the level of incompetence of the treating physicians brings so much of disappointment amongst the patients and to their family members that they do not feel like going to the hospital any more. Such type of apathy towards the system have brought a great deal of bad name to the doctors and the hospital but seemed to have very little effect on their day to day functioning. It was evident that the people were also not confident enough to take their patients to these hospital. Rather, they resort to supernatural power.

The Communicable Diseases

The study revealed that like any other health problems the people of the area were also the victims of various types of chromic diseases. Some of the common chronic diseases wer asthma, skin diseases, pharyngitis, and various types of upper and lower respiratory tract inflections (URI) and (LRI).

But it was noted that most common and widely prevalent problem of the area was asthma. As it was commonly reported by the residents, according to them disease was mostly found amongst the adults and exacerbate during the seasonal change. An attempt was made to understand meaning, perception and the way patient and relatives react to the disease of asthma. One of the respondent from block-K called Amir Chand readily told his own experience as he was ailing for last twenty years of asthma. He narrated his own problem in the following words.

> Initially when he was suffering of the problem of asthma it was not known to him or to the doctors, he used to go and complain of breathing trouble with intermittent cough. The doctors who were treating him used to give expectorant and sedatives so that he could sleep well at night, as he had complained of sleepless nights due to asthma.
>
> As the problem continued he requested doctors of the locality to refer him to the hospital. As soon as he approached the hospital he was given admission in the hospital because the day he had gone to get admission he was gasping for breath. They had put an Oxygen mask on his face and gave some injection too, then only he got relief. He was admitted to Hindu Rao initially and was kept for four days and out of those four days once he was taken to Intensive Care Unit (ICU).
>
> He was released from the hospital on the fifth day and he was told by the doctor that if at all he suffers of asthmatic bout any more then he can visit the OPD. But as the reluctance of the Hindu Rao staff increased gradually after each visit, and no medicines were given to him at times, he stopped going there (this behaviour was very common in the dispensary of the hospital, most of the time it was said that the medicine is out of stock). But only positive thing in the hospital was that they prescribed seven days medicine, out of which he had to buy four days medicine.
>
> But the trouble was of standing in the queue and wastage of time waiting used to be so long that he did not like going there. He pleaded for a separate OPD for asthmatic patient like that of heart patient while narrating the episode, he thinks otherwise the patients will have to suffer quite a lot.
>
> On asking about the patient's troubles while admitted at Intensive Care Unit (ICU). The respondent said,
>
> He was gasping severely when he was admitted to ICU, but due to paucity of Oxygen cylinder, he was about to collapse. The nurses were unable to manage cylinder. He was lucky that a senior doctor had come on round at that time and he had himself managed the Oxygen cylinder for him.

These things show that even in ICUs the patients are not fully safe. Patient could collapse due to lack of essential things like Oxygen. This showed that the nurses as well as the ward boys were not alert nither proactive for procuring things in advance.

Chronic Aliment

The cases of chronic ailments clearly showed the various erratic behaviour of the patient. Moreover, the chronic diseases of skin destroys the whole routine of the patient. It is not fatalistic but quite vexing. The common diseases which were found in the colony were dermatitis, fungal infection, besides, various rashes of skin and skin allergy. It was found that skin ailment had some affinity with economic status of the people. Moreover, the general hygiene of the area was by and large of sub-standard in nature which lead to various types of skin diseases. In some cases, the problem of Angular Stomatis was also reported, caused due to deficiency of Vitamin-B Complex.

A particular case of Mr. Razak of Block-C was studied in detail in order to know about the various problems the poor people face in the area particularly with respect to skin problem. Razak narrated his case in the following way:-

> ......with the increase in severity of the problem, he used to frequent to the local dispensary to get cured. He was always given a tablet which used to make him feel drowsy. But as long as he remained awake he felt irritation on whole body surface. After couple of visits he was also given a lotion to apply topically. The lotion was helpful for him for few days but again the problem aggravated.
>
> Thereafter, he was referred to Hindu Rao by the dispensary doctor. The doctor at skin OPD prescribed medicine but as Razak went to take medicine at the dispensary of the hospital, he was told medicine was out of stock but he was lucky enough to get the same medicine from local dispensary after three days. Although, the medicine gave some relief for a month or so but itching started once again after a month. At that time one of the neighbours suggested him to visit to St. Stephen, skin OPD, he was quite disturbed and he sincerely visited to St. Stephens. There the doctor at OPD gave patience hearing to him. The doctor also asked about his profession. He told that his profession was garbage picking. The doctor told him if he could change his profession then there is chance of getting his skin disease cured. He expressed his inability to change his profession.

> But he had insisted to the doctor to give him some medicine which could cure him without change of his profession. The doctor did give him a medicine which was supposed to be affective.
>
> As he could not purchase the medicine he was given free of charge but to confirm his income status, the Medical Social Worker of the hospital visited his house and confirmed his real status and then only he was given the free medicine for sometimes. But, they did not give him medicine for longer period so he had to go to market to purchase medicine for himself. But, as he could not continue to purchase medicine of his own, his skin condition deteriorated. Gradually, he leamt to live with pain. Earlier, he had itching on legs only but of late he had problems of hand and back as well...

This showed that most of the skin diseases were linked with hygiene of the individual and the hygienic condition to a large extent is connected with the economic status of the individual. As mortality due to the skin disease was not high, the urgency to handle the ailment on urgent basis was never warrented.

So far as the allergy of skin was concerned, a detailed narrative of Savitri Devi of Bhalasawa village, who was suffering of serious skin allergy, has been given below.

> She developed rash on her neck and armpit whenever she took spinach, curd and brinjal the magnitude of the suffering increased particularly before and durning summer. She had gone to Kasturba Gandhi hospital to get treated, the doctor told her not take those food stuffs which were responsible for allergy. And also prescribed some medicine. She continued with that medicine although, she got some relief with the medicine for a year or so. But, she found that after two years she had developed allergy from ghee as well.
>
> Once again she visited the skin OPD, the doctor told her to stop ghee also. After a year's time she developed allergy for rice as well and she had to give up rice too. After getting fed up with so much of food taboos, she decided to undergo thorough check up in the hospital, but as she requested for thorough check up, she was not cared and nobody histened her. She went to the hospital at least four to five times but all in vain.
>
> Finally, she had caught hold of a senior government official through whom she pressurised the Medical Superintendent and he in turn asked senior doctor to treat her and also asked for all sorts of check ups, i.e., stool, blood, urine and other very many tests. But, unfortunately, they could

> not come to any conclusion. During the whole process her daughter's study got badly affected, as a result she failed in her examination. And Savitri Devi did not get cure as well. she remained, as she was.
>
> After all these ordeal, she stopped going to any doctor but she went to a baba, who was supposed to cure all sorts of skin disease. And with the various instructions of baba, besides his medicine she started getting relief. And baba told her that she would be totally cured in due course of time....

The above incidence clearly showed that most of the chronic skin diseases were non-curable by modern allopathic medicine.

Leukorrhea complain was common amongst the women, particularly in the resettlement colony. The common complaint by every lady patient who had been suffering of leukorrhea was that they had been visiting to local dispensary but did not get any relief from the alopathic medicine. Even the OPD treatment of Kasturba Gandhi as well other hospitals did not give any relief to the patients. To get relief they stopped going to allopathic hospitals, on the contrary they were visiting to the Ayurvedic hospital. And all those women had been visiting to the ayurvedic hospital and they also reported of relief in the ayurvedic treatment and medicine. Even those chronic cases who had been suffering for more than a year got lot of relief after they started going to the ayurvedic dispensary or the hospital. This claim of cure of ayurvedic treatment of leukorrhea was also confirmed by the doctors of the Allopathic medicine without any hesitation.

It was clear from the above studies that in cases of chronic ailment the allopathic system was not able to handle the cases after certain limit but it was not openly accepted by most of the doctors. In such situation, the patient kept on moving from one place to the other with hope that they would get cured sometimes, but when they would be cured they did not know, after getting frustated from clinical shopping time and again. they became highly apathetic towards the whole system of allopathy and became antagonistic to it. Whereas, it was noted that chronic cases of all kinds (chronicity due to clinical misjudgment of the cases though not always sheer negligence of the patient leading to chronicity) could never be cured by allopathic doctors on the contrary the ayurvedic treatment proved relatively better and efficacious in many circumstances.

Accidents and Various Other Mishaps

Occurrence of accident was so high amongst the residents of the area during the study period almost one case of accident was reported every day. Majority of the worker were engaged in one or the other factory doing various kinds of hard and risky work. Some of them were working as daily wage earner in textile mills and some of them were in foundries. Mainly due to two reasons they used to meet with accident in their work place. (a) Reluctance to carry out the work as per the directives given in work place. (b) Ill-kept and malfunctioning plants which were rarely maintained by the owner, in order to save money, mostly lead to serious accidents. In very few cases, the over-enthusiastic workers, in order to earn more, worked inspite of fatigue and finally met with accidents.

Mr. Rikhi Lal who was worker in Rajasthan Udyog Ltd. working in spinning plant. He was sitting at home with a big bandage wrapped round his arm. The scholar asked the reason of bandage round his arm and he told the incidence in the following words.

> ....He was working in night shift in a textile mill but all of a sudden the roller stopped, even then the mill was functioning but within half an hour's time the mill stopped functioning altogether. There were not many people around, so he could not call any people in the factory but alone tried to check up the switch box to find out the fault in the box but he found that it was perfectly alright. Then he checked the roller manually. And all of a sudden the roller became operational and in a fraction of a second the roller broke his arm bone, although he was quick enough to pull back his arms though he succeded but he fell unconscious.
>
> After regaining consciousness he found himself in Hindu Rao hospital. His wife was by his side and he was connected with a drip line. He was released from Hindu Rao after ten days stay. He was told by the co-workers that the owner was bearing all the expenses for his hospitalisation, doctor and medicine. But in the hospital, the nurses were always rude to him and to his wife, they always used to make them feel that they were doing a great obligation to him by keeping him admitted. The ward *aya* and the ward boy were not rude to them but reluctant to help, as soon as they realised the patient was not in position to give tips to them. Although, the doctor visited him but just for few minutes and used to ask about well being very casually.
>
> His wife faced lot of problems, if she were to ask lunch or dinner for herself. The ward boys used to refuse to give her lunch or dinner and it was only after lot of persuation she could get food. They were helpless and had to listen unpleasent talks to get extra meal. Later on, he realised

that such humiliation was due to non- entitlement of food for the attendants.

As soon as he was discharged he had visited the Basaidhara Pur E.S.I. Hospital. As children were small, they could not be sent to fetch his medicine and his wife had to look after the domestic chores most of the time. It became problematic for him, he requested the doctors that if, they could admit him in the hospital. After considering the case, they decided to give him a bed for two days. He was treated thereafter in the hospital. But this time he had problem with his own food. They used to give him every thing as per the prescription but for eggs which was also there in the diet list but the diet was served without egg. Even, though he complained about it to the doctor but the doctor did not do anything. Thereafter, the doctor did not make it a big issue. Another problem which he faced in ESI was of the class IV staffs behaviour and attitude towards him.

They were always on look out for some money or some tips even if they were asked to do small favours.

During his stay at ESI the doctor had asked him for blood, after his group was detected the doctor enquired about the same from the blood bank but the reply was in negative. So, he had to go to market to purchase blood. Later on a patient next to his bed told him blood was available for those patients who payed for it or had good contact and could pass few words through the medical superintendent to the blood bank incharge .

Moreover, he found that on the third day of his stay his bed was allotted to a six year old boy, who had fracture of lower limb. As Rikhi Lal had resisted initially for it, he was told that he would be discharged in case he has problem to share the bed. Even, though he did not make much noise about it, on the fifth day morning the doctor told him that he was perfectly alright and will be discharged by the evening of the same day. But, he realised one thing in the process of his stay that one should not show ones anger or grudge when admitted in the ward otherwise, he would be thrown off in no time. He was also convinced that if any body of lower economic status wants treatment, then he or she should surrender totally and should not ask embarrassing questions to doctors or nurses. The class IVs were nice to him to talk but they never helped easily until or unless they were assured that they would have some extra cash or kind from the patient or the patient's relatives....

If Mr. Rikhi Lal was also asked about incidences of preferential treatment, if he had come across any, while admitted in the hospital. The respondent told the following things about preferential treatment.

There was one patient next to his bed in Hindu Rao, for him doctors used to come thrice a day. The visitors to the patient used to come by car. The attendant of the patient and others were very demanding type but nobody checked the attendant, the staffs complied with whatever the attendant asked to them, which was not true in case of Rikhi Lal. A brief conversation with the fellow patients during the stay in the hospital, Rikhi Lal realised that the fellow patient was a friend of the Deputy Medical Superintendent, of the hospital, as a result the Medical Superintendent accompanied with the deputy often visited him and enquired about his health. But nobody had bothered about Rikhi Lal or others patients.

The above incidence showed that a patient could be entitled for many things but he may not get it. Moreover, if patient does not know about his rights while admitted in the hospitals whether in Babu Jagtiban Ram, Hindu Rao or E.S.I. He would not receive treatment as per his requirement. The preferential treatment becomes more conspicuous when the next bed patient is cared extra ordinarily or favoured just because he has contacts with the high ups of the hospital. It also proves that parochialism towards patients was wide spread. Although, no one of the staffs, of the hospital were ready to admit that the favouritism to some or parochialism to some is being done by them quite often.

As the cases of burns were also common, it became equally important to know that how the cases were being taken care of at local level as well as what sort of treatment being given to those who were visiting hospital. As the cases of burning were typical in themselves so it was necessary to know perception of the people regarding those cases.

The Burns and Injuries

Munna a two year old child had third, degree of burn on his leg and body. His mother was asked to narrate the case.

> "Munna was sleeping, his mother had gone out to purchase vegetables in the lane in front of the house only. But, in the mean time he got up and as the boy could not find her mother so started searching through out the house. The stove was burning in full flames. The child did not notice that and collided with it and got himself burnt.
>
> He could not bear the pain and was screaming, she got totally bewildered at the episode, she took him to the doctor in the Babu Jagjiban Ram

> Memorial hospital. The doctor immediately referred him to Kasturba OPD. She went there immediately, somehow he was admitted in I.C.U. He was treated at I.C.U. for three days. They gave him all sorts of medicines except for one ointment, which she had to purchase from the market. But by the fourth day, he was transferred to general ward of pediatrics department. By then, she had observed degree of variation in treatment pattern. The nurses were mostly reluctant to tell anything more than once, they always talked in a dictating tone. One nurse was really too bad she used to taunt her.
>
> The cleanliness and the hygiene of the ward was not at all good. The milk which was brought for the children was mostly spoiled by the stray cat of the ward. Similarly in the wards particularly, if, the child was asleep and the attendant was away the cats used to drink the milk. Although, she once told this to ward *aya* and the nurse but both of them had paid deaf ear to it. Realising the situation she stopped giving the hospital milk to the child, she used to get milk from her house only. But many children were taking hospital milk inspite of knowing the fact that the milk is contaminated. Her son was discharged after tenth day from the hospital and the day he was discharged two children were allotted the same bed. But later the son was taken for private treatment, as she could not go to Kasturba OPD after every three or four days, Even with the private medication the son was recuperating day by day but the only problem she faced was the cost of the medicines....

This shows that as long as the patient was admitted in intensive care unit the patients had some hope of getting better treatment, medicine and food as well but as soon as they were transferred to general ward everything went wrong. The behaviour also changed towards the patient. And the change was applicable in all cases and in all age groups and sex. On the whole, it was clear that there was a great degree of apathy which prevails in the mind of the staffs towards the patient, they were taken as burden and nobody remains committed to the Hippocratic oath which they take when they join this nobel profession.

Sanitation and Hygiene of the Colony

To understand the health culture of the people of the colony and the village, it was equally important to know the environmental sanitation of the area which is responsible for well being of the people of the area, i.e. the general hygiene of the locality and the lanes and the drains which run left and right through the colony and through the village, and the filth or garbage on the lanes or in the drains which became breeding ground for all sorts of flies and mosquitoes. Logging of drains and gutters causing all sorts of nuisance for the people of the area. While moving around the colony or the village unhygienic conditions were evinced. The situation got exacerbated by free movement of stray animals all over the colony and in the village. This type of background helped foster ample amount of vectors of the diseases, resulting in various diseases like, malaria, Japanese encephalitis (JE) and Dengu. Various worm born diseases were also very common i.e. intestinal worms, pin worms and tape worms.

Sanitation and Hygiene of the individual and the surroundings are inalienable from of health of the locals. Although, apparently relations may not look clear and distinct. It must be also mentioned in this context that it is difficult for the poor people to maintain hygiene by themselves, as it can not be maintained without spending money. They were hardly able to mange two square of meals in a normal situation, so they could not think of spending their hard earned money for maintenance of hygiene and sanitation of the surroundings. The hygienic and sanitary condition of the people of the resettlement and that of the village had direct bearing on their health culture. So, an opinion about the sanitary and hygienic condition of the colony was collected from the residents of the colony and the village.

Table 5.23 shows that amongst the poor twenty six percent of the people said that sanitary condition of the people were fair in Jahangirpuri. Nearly seventy four percent of the poor said that the sanitary condition of the resettlement colony was very bad. So far as the complains of unsanitary and unhygenic condition of the colony was concerned, the residents had many complaints, some of the common complains of the poor were, the gutters and their lanes never got cleaned those were filthy and stinky or chocked with all sorts of garbage and the situation used to deteriorate in rainy seasons, during those days walking through the lanes became next to impossible as the lanes overflew. The poor people also said that whenever the municipality workers came for cleaning they did not listen the locals and they did not take care of the actual problem they did whatever they felt necessary. Given all these conditions the poor of the area to a large extent had accepted the status of environment as normal, thereby, denying for themselves any move to form any kind of pressure group by which they could get their work done in the colony for their own betterment.

Table: 5.23

Distribution Showing the Assessment of Sanitation of the Study Area by Three Strata

Income Group	*Fair*	*V.Bad*
Poor	25	70
	(26.31)	(73.68)
Middle	20	146
	(12.04)	(87.9)
Rich	9	45
	(16.66)	(83.33)
Total	54/315	261/315

Amongst, the middle class only twelve percent said that the sanitary and the hygienic condition of the colony were fair. Whereas, almost eighty eight percent of the middle income group said it was very bad. Other than those complains made by the poor, the middle income group threw the blame of such aweful situation on their poorer co-inhabitants. Moreover, they also said that the mushroom growth of various temples hindered the construction of public latrines, as a result the children of most of the colony dwellers defecated on the roadside. As a result the roads became unwalkable both in summer and rainy seasons.

Amongst the rich, seventeen percent of the people said that the sanitary condition of the colony was not up to the mark. And the scholar found that these seventeen percent were those people who were not first of all concerned with the colony because they hardly stayed over there. And even if they were staying, they got everything for themselves by giving money to the sweepers, to the chowkidars and other "safai workers".

Whereas, eighty three percent of the rich said that sanitary condition of the colony was very bad. One of the rich residents Mr. Ram Lal told the scholar about the colony and its hygienic condition in the following words.

> Majority of well to do people were migrant to this area, they had taken the plots from the original allottee by means of power of attorney. Allottees were paid good amount of premium on the actual price of the plot at that time (nearly twenty years ago). Initially, they thought that the colony would come up like other colonies of Delhi and the government authorities

will look more into its affairs. But their calculation failed because the area remained neglected by the authorities.

The above mentioned situation clearly showed that the overall situation of the colony hardly improved because the poor remained neglected. In reality the poor lacked both the political and economic power to mobilise things to get better deal.

Middle income group were so fussy in nature regarding the sanitation and hygiene of their locality that whenever, they wanted to take joint action for the betterment of the area their religion, caste, language came on their way, ultimately things did not move forward. Moreover, many of them were selling off their plot so, they did not think in terms of inproving the sanitary and hygienic condition of the colony.

The rich were not concerned with overall improvement of hygiene and sanitation because they were able to keep their surrounding clean by paying. By and large it was found that the very basic objective of the resettlement to a large extent got defeated, as one of the inherent element of this rehabilitation was to give them better living condition then slum, but which in reality could not be provided. On the contrary these dwellings were giving rise to new kind of concrete slums, which were more permanent in nature in comparison to their erstwhile counterparts.

The physical and mental health is not only related with psychosomatic ailment or the sanitary and hygienic condition of the colony but also with the working environment of the people. i.e. the type of job, working hours, mental satisfaction in the job and situation of the working space. Hard and demanding work compelled these people to become addict of one or the other type of toxicant. It was noted that amongst the poorer section around thirty percent were alcoholic. And so far as the consumption of alcohol was concerned right from local brew to standard alcohol, everything they consumed. Mainly the lathe machine workers and heavy vehicle drivers were fond of taking hard drinks. Remaining twenty of thirty percent of these workers took drink but they were very casual drinkers. Or in other words, they consumed drink once or twice in a month. It was also observed from amongst these drinking lot, around five percent of these people were drug addicts, mainly of brown sugar and ninety percent of these consumers were auto rickshaw drivers. They were initiated to substance abuse due to their peer pressure to begin with and later on they hooked on to it.

Alcoholism and Health Problems

In chapter-3, it was stated that alcoholism amongst youth and others was one of the common features of the colony. It was present amongst all section of the population.

Some of the addicts started alcohol very casually but it became part and parcel of their life. As all these things had direct bearing on the health culture of the people so, it was necessary to know the magnitude of alcohol consumption of the people in this area.

Table 5.24 shows that amongst the poor people nearly eight percent were regular taker of alcohol. They consumed liquor every day. Forty two percent of the poor were moderate drinker, in other words these people consumed drink at least ten to fifteen days a months. And four percent were taking alcohol once in a month or once in a two months. And a sizeable number, of near about forty five percent said they had not taken alcohol any time. But on the whole, the number of consumers were more than the non-consumers among the poor. In other words, it can be said that drinking was not looked down upon in the poverty stricken society. People had accepted it as matter of enjoyment and pleasure rather than a constant economic drainage. But, it is also clear that they had no leeway to alcohol abuse.

Table: 5.24

Distribution Showing Pattern of Alcohol Consumption in Three Strata

Income Group	*Regular Consumer*	*Moderate Consumer*	*Casual Consumer*	*Do Not Take*
Poor	8	40	4	43
	(8.42)	(42.10)	(4.21)	(45.2)
Middle	6	55	10	95
	(3.61)	(33.13)	(6.02)	(57)
Rich	4	7	9	34
	(7.40)	(4.21)	(16.66)	(62.9)
Total	18/315	102/315	23/315	172/315

Amongst the middle class more than three and a half percent were regular drinker. Around thirty three percent were moderate drinkers. And six percent of the people in this category were casual drinker. In this category, fifty seven percent of the people did not drink at all or they had never tasted any kind of alcohol.

Amongst the richer section of the population nearly seven percent of the people were regular alcoholics. Only four percent were moderate drinker of alcohol. And, nearly seventeen percent were casual drinkers. And a majority, more than sixty percent did not take or have not taken alcohol any time in their life time.

It also became clear from the above table that casual drinkers were more in percentage i.e. thirty three percent. Whereas rest of the drinkers were both regular and casual type. But the total percentage of drinkers did not exceed forty five percent. Rest of the population were non drinkers.

The consumption of liquor also consists of the local contraband drink known as "gattoo", which was sold only to known people in absolute disguise, in a hush hush manner. The study showed that police personnel knew about it but they did not say anything as they were getting share out of the deal.

So far as smoking habit of the people is concerned it was found that more than ninety five percent of household were of smoker's (comprising of both the resettlement and the village). Amongst these smokers only 2/3 percent of the women were smoking. In the process of tobacco smoking, they (around five percent) gradually caught on with smack and brown sugar (although not all of them). The unfortunate situation is that they did not have any doctor who would treat them, nor did they have any rehabilitation centre for these people.

Consumption of "pan" (beetle leaf) was mostly confound within the Muslim families in most of the cases, with some exception of the Hindus as well. Although, the general convention goes that too much of pan chewing with tobacco leads to oral cancer, however such a case was not found amongst the consumers of pan and tabacco during the study neither did the doctors of the colony confirm it. But it is more than clear that those who were taking pan regularly were having very bad and weak denture.

Regular drinking of alcohol and hooch caused immense loss of money, energy and time of these people. The ematiated bodies of alcoholics could not bear the brunt of heavy and arduous work, so at home also most of the manual jobs were done by the women of the house. The alcoholics in many cases were observed to have lost appetite and were in bad shape.

In some cases, they vomited so badly that no solid food could be retaind by them, which ultimately led to severe weakness and irritability amongst the alcoholics. Moreover, they proved menace for their wife and children (during hangover they assaulted their wife and children for no good reason).

They were equally hated by the colony people as they created nuisance by making lot of noise during the odd hours of the night. It was also observed that smoking and drinking were done in most of the cases, which made the addicts not only ematiated but also made them prone to various infection of lung and respiratory tract, besides, damaging their liver. On enquiring in details about family reaction towards the alcoholics from Laxmi, wife of Chote Lal a private bus driver, she told,

> Her husband was totally drunk and lying unconscious in the bus stop for whole night, whereas, they were worried and had no information about him. Her husband was lying unconscious in one of the bus stops of G.T. Kamal Road which runs in front of the colony. Next morning he was brought home by a police man and his face was full of bruises. The police had told her that the cuts on his face was due to collision with the iron pillars at the bus stop (while he was drunk he collided there). But as soon as the police man had left, her husband told that he was taken to custody by the patrol police and he was bitten there. He was only released when he had given whatever money he had in his pocket to the officer who were beating him....

The above case showed that Chote Lal not only suffered himself but created problem for his family as well. So far as the consumption of drugs were concerned it was found that the addicts were primarily frustated and dejected. They had no job and they were being nagged at home, even if they had source of earning the income was not sufficient to run the family. To get rid of such problems they started consuming drug and became addict. On meeting Faridas brother (vide case study of chapter 3) it was found that he was weak and had a feeling of insecurity and was lacking self confidence. He mostly skipped lunch or dinner as he never felt hungry due to loss of appetite. He was suffering of cough and cold, as well as dizziness. He suffered of tremendous withdrawal syndrome i.e. vomiting, body and headache, uneasyness and at times loose motions in the absence of substance of abuse. And it was unfortunate that he had no one to sympathise or no organisation to give him a viable alternative to get over the withdrawal and to lead a normal life after giving up drug.

People's Perception of Local Health Care Institution and Hospitals

The people of this area were frequenting to the local health care institutions but mostly remained unsatisfied as they used to-get worked up in long queue even to meet the doctor and get prescription. Even, if, they were able to meet the doctor he gave them a very brief hearing and wrote such a prescription that the dispensary could not provide even half or two third of the prescribed medicines. So, they had to purchase the rest of it from the chemists shop. Given such a background they mostly preferred to go to private practitioners, where by paying they were able to get rid of all sorts of botheration, even could save the loss of days wage. Some of the residents visited to OPD's of various hospitals i.e. Babu Jagjiban Ram, Hindu Rao, St. Stephens. All these hospitals being general hospital, all sorts of cases visited there. In the OPD, they always found lots of rush that made them either to bear with the pain and wait for the turn or leave the OPD without getting treatment. Sometimes, their turn would come so late that the doctor would leave the seat as his duty hours were over by that time, in such condition the patient remained unchecked and untreated inspite of his pains and sufferings and long wait. The casualty and emergency unit of Babu Jagjiban Ram or Hindu Rao rarely accepted a case but for the severe or terminal ones were accepted. The treatment in those two units were better than the indoor wards, as facilities provided in these units were of better nature. Even, if the people got admission they were treated in a very inhuman way or in other words the empathy of the doctor and the nurse was always missing in these units. So far as the behaviour of the staffs were concerned it was observed that staffs were rude to talk to them, things were smoother and easier only when there existed prior acquaintance or some payments made i.e. tips were given to these people (to the class-IV, in particular) in one or the other form. So far as St. Stephens was concerned patients said that the OPD in this hospital was much more systematic and less time consuming than Kasturba or Hindu Rao or Babu Jagjiban Ram. But in St. Stephens also, one need to pay to get good medicines (which would give quick relief). The OPD card holders were only referred to indoor. The general hygiene of the wards were better than the MCD hospitals. The nurses were nice to talk and the class-IV staffs were never given any bribe as it was strictly against the rule. But, it was felt by the patients that there exists preferential treatment for the Christian patients. The doctors were stratified in terms of their payment, in other words to visit the senior and reputed doctor for treatment, one had to pay the high fees. But on the whole the extremely poor remained neglected in this hospital too.

For Kasturba the patients of the area said that the OPD was too crowded and lacked any kind of sanitation and hygiene. The medicine preseribed in OPD were mostly not available. The patient said the cases of family planning viz, tubectomy were dealt efficiently but the post operation complications were not sincerely taken care of. The indoor facility was not bad but the availability of drug and a sympathetic doctor as well as helpful nature of staffs were very rare. The emergency and the casualty were better in terms of functioning but with a slight improvement in the condition of the patient of emergency or casualty, he is pushed to general ward and the situation once again become aweful. The class-IVs staffs were very rude and they fleeced off the patient particularly in the gynae ward, if the new-born is a boy child the staffs are crazy to earn some tips. Babu Jagjiban Ram hospital is though run by Delhi Administration. But the health care quality was no better than that of Hindu Rao or Kasturba hospitals. The rush, the untidiness of the hospital combined with rude behaviour of the doctors and staff often disheartened the patients of the colony and the village. As most of the colony dwellers and villagers had pinned their hopes on this hospital, even before it came into existance. But the functioning of this hospital did not come upto their expectations. Many a time the patients abuse the hospital in totality and its staffs in the same language, as they used for other government hospitals.

The only positive aspect of treatment in Babu Jagjiban Ram was the proximity of the hospital for resettlers and the villagers. They did not waste time to communte nor did they spend for transport. This hospitals is frequented by the local at any point of time for treatment that also rendereds the local dispensaries to a large extent less functional or made it a less functioning entity.

The patient had apathy towards the excessive crowd and unsanitary condition of the hospitals in general. According to them hospitals could be defined as,

(A) It is a place to get treated by staying there.
- A place where medicine and food both are given.
- Once admitted can get treated by various gadgets and doctors.
- Almost everyone said that number of staffs were inadequate to

serve the patients better.

(B) Moreover, they also perceived the hospital, in negative sense they complained of,

- Admission in hospital was difficult.
- Lack of bed was common.
- Inadequate and bland diet (except in St. Stephens) were given to patient.
- Rough behaviour with attendants (except in St. Stephens) of the patients.
- Lack of blood bottles during operation.
- Absence of proper guidance i.e. arrow mark or written instruction, by which patient can be facilitated.
- Untowards behaviour towards the patients when they arrived for follow-up.
- Scarcity of logistics were also reported. On the whole, it was realised that the local health care institution and hospitals have lot of scope to improve in order to become a people's institution. At the same time, it was found that the hospitals have been seen as independent secluded indentity in itself. The society or the community at large visualised the hospital something as alien and not an integral part of their community or scoiety. Irony of such a thinking is mutual exclusion, non-commital and unaccountable functioning combined with rise in frustation of the people, as the expectations remain unmet. To meet the unmet felt need, to make institution more user friendly, there is a need to make these institution absolutely socially acceptable in structure and function.

6

ISSUES AND CHALLENGES

On the basis of the study of the culture of the resettlers and the villagers of Bhalasawa, it can be asserted that there is not much of cultural trait difference between the two cultures but both are distinct in their manifestation of cultural expressions. However, the determinants of the two cultures (village and resettlement) are governed by the dynamics of the local socio-political and economic modalities.

In fact, there is considerable concern among the social scientists about the approach to study the culture of slum dwellers or resettlers or the sub-urban villages. Culture of these people are contingent upon various intervention of complex urbanisation process. Various sub-cultural groups of resettlement colony and the village Bhalasawa provided a very good opportunity to study the dynamics of changes in the health and culture of the resettlers and the villagers.

Compared to urban living, living in sub-urban villages or resettlement colonies has major disadvantages. A big city enjoys many social, economic and political benefits that are not available to a population of corresponding size in sub-urban villages or resettlement colony. The dependence of the resettlers and sub-urban villages on big cities makes them more vulnerable to exploitation and are in complete control of city-based political leaders, industrialists, traders, bureaucrats, and intellectuals. For instance, a person living in a resettlement colony or in a sub-urban village becomes seriously ill, he has very limited access (both physical and economical) to the hospital services. The hospital facilities being complex and complicated often, he may have to visit to a near by private practitioner for easier and less complicated investigation and treatment procedure to avoid complications. Even, when physicians at the hospital are able to handle the problem with more reasonable confidence, the relatives might have to rush to get special medicines for the patient that might have been prescribed by the physician, this means wastage of their time, effort, and money needed to undertake the journey to bring medicine, besides, relative is more prone to be cheated by the medicine sellers in terms of price and genuinity of the medicine. Meanwhile, the patient starts languishing in the foreign atmosphere, as he is not versed with hospital set up.

And the patient has to learn various hospital based stress coping mechanism. This makes the situation even more complex. The relative in many ocassion is incompetent to handle both the patient and the doctor at a time. Becuase, he is also new to such a sitution.

In contrast, a well-off city dweller in Delhi has relatively easier access to sophisticated medical institution and good quality medicines with less expense and effort. While a rickshaw-puller staying in the resettlement colony or sub-urban village in the same city, may not be able to derive the same degree of benefits, but faces distinct disadvantages to achieve meaningful health services at the time of his need. As he is not well adapted with living skills, like his city cousine. This skill is not only required to acquire the health services but also in meeting the basic needs of day to life process.

The health culture of a population includes cultural perception and cultural meaning of various health problems, the various cultural mechanisms that are adopted by the community to deal with such problems, the various purposive interventions by the government in the field of health and the behaviour of individuals in response to the various health problems. The pre-existing health culture of a population is also to be understood in the context of the cultural dynamics.

The people who have been resettled in various resettlement colonies of Delhi have experienced the various life process while staying earlier in authorised and unauthorised slums, after, migrating from various rural pockets of different states, while migrating to Delhi, they have carried their cultural traits and their earlier health culture. During their stay in the slum battering of slum life forced them to loose some of their earlier cultural values as well as health culture. They started adopting slowly to the new forms of health practices under compulsion, in an alien culture. Subsequently, their pre-existing health culture vis-a-vis their present culture gave the whole complex a new form. The new form of health culture of these resettlers in the resettlement colony is the core of the present study, the study has been designed to know the dynamics of cultural change; viz, a shift from village life to slum life and finally slum to resettlement.

To understand this change the present way of life of these resettlers has to be understood, which has been affected heavily by contaminated food and drinking water, dust, dirt and infestations by various kinds of insects and other pests and parasites, extensive poverty, grossly substandard housing, poor drainage and fecal contamination of the soil and extremely poor personal hygiene. These togather creates an ecological condition highly conducive to widespread prevalence of various kinds of communicable diseases, undernutrition and malnutrition and high rate of morbidity and mortality among children and mothers, combined with the health hazards caused by accidents in these localities. Unlike the main city dweller who enjoys more privilege living in better hygenic condition and enjoying more civic amenities through his political, economic and social connections.

The abject dependence of resettlement on the authorised adjoining colonies and the flanking village life have profound influence on the culture of the resettlement including the health culture of inhabitants of Jahangirpuri. This influence is more pronounced amongst the poorer sections. They suffer from deprivations because they are poor, because they have lower rates of literacy, and because they are totally dependent on the richer section of the adjoning colonies and succeptible to exploitation. This denial of social justice and political rights restricts opportunities and facilities needed to bring about cultural changes and to cope more effectively with various problems. Often this adverse conditions of the poor make them cling to ideas and practices which are blatently obscuratant in nature. It must be noted that these determinants of culture are quite different from what are generally included under "culture of poverty". For a proper understanding of the cultural practices of a community including its health practice it is, necessary to relate its culture to the social, economic and political forces which maintain the ecological settings. Out of the most striking findings of this study, the extensive prevalence of poverty conbined with frustation and helplessness was very clearly evident. Poverty also leads to further disintegration and deterioration of the environment and of living condition, sanitation, of the quality of drinking water, of shelter, of clothing, and so forth.

This unequal settlement pattern and living conditions, making the inhabitants of Jahangirpuri and Bhalasawa village dependent on the unfavourable ecological conditions, leading to exploitation and social injustice and extensive poverty, which has far reaching influence on the — entire way of life of the ressettlement, all such considerations shapes cultural perception and cultural meaning of health problems and people's response to health services provided by the hospitals and local dispenseries. Furthermore, it would be simplistic to consider the cultural traits as static entities. Though, in their efforts, — or struggle — people seek out new way of perceiving their health problems and their cultural meaning, along with such changes they also develop better ways of coping with their health problems, by formulating or searching out new health institutions (private practitioners) and changing, their health behaviour. This understanding is central to the present study.

It was observed in the present study that system of institutional health care in operation in that area was complex rather than a simple one. It has been noted that the ex-practitioner of Hindu Rao hospital are leading (private) practitioners of the resettlement colony, who at times conceal their incapability to treat a case by sending the patients to Hindu Rao, which not only gets them high esteem in the eyes of the patient but also helps sustain the professional link of the doctor with his ex-colleagues.

Such kind of referral is beneficial for the patient, as he can get preferential treatment in terms of jumping the queue, taking more and more time from the referred doctor for consultation, getting better and effective medicine prescribed by the doctor and at times patients get all or most of the prescribed medicines free of cost from the hospital itself.

These kinds of favours to the patient in turn becomes beneficial for the doctor to carry out the private practice.

The patient who approaches straight to the doctor in the hospital and gets treated in O.P.D. or tries to get admission may not get many simple and ordinary help which a known patient will get. Even, if the patient is admitted he faces a lot of humiliation during his stay both in the hands of doctors and other staff. Such humiliation is mostly the outcome of highly bureaucratised and technocratic, non humanistic health care system of various government institutations.

Majority of the hospital O.P.D. cases are non-referral whereas such visits to hospital is non-welcome situation, contrary it increases utter confusion in the working of the hospital. The massive load of unguided patients not only create a huge rush in the O.P.D. but also most of the time patients remain inadequately served.

This type of chaos can be avoided by proper referral and by imparting adequate knowledge about the function and meaning of the hospital. Moreover, there is need of thorough guidance and instruction for the people and patient to make these institutions purposefully effective.

It was also reported by the nurses of Babu Jagjiban Ram Memorial hospital that less than five percent of the patients visiting from Jahangirpuri belong to richer section of the population, even majority of that five percent is comprised of patients from the village of Bhalasawa (app. 3% belong to village).

It was noted that the delivery of child of the resettlement colony were mostly conducted at Kasturba Gandhi hospital, on querying from the nurses and the doctors, it was found that the villagers of Bhalasawa did not visit the M.C.D. dispensaries or Babu Jagjiban Ram hos 1 pital or for that matter to Kasturba hospital (inspite of local referrals), due to low standard of hygiene and over crowded bed situation. The fact of untidiness was also endorsed by some of the nurses in a very technical manner viz;

In other words, they said the chances of nosocomial cross-infection was high because of duplication and triplication of patients in a single bed. Moreover, it was found that the patients were lying on the floors and on the corridors for days together. The uncleanliness became more glaring while it was observed that the cats were loitering right within each and every ward and fiddling with the medicine or the food of the patient in their absence or when the patient was sleeping. On asking about the menace of cat in the wards, one of the nurses told that, "these cats mainly survived on the thrown away placenta of the patient, once they got the taste of it they are not likely to leave the ward and the hospital." The suffering does not end there. The menace of stray monkey was equally disturbing. The panic on the corridors were due to encroachment of monkey on the corridors and in some odd cases inside the ward as well. The monkey bite is as fatal as dog because these apes also carry the virus of rabies.

About the standard of treatment the nurses showed a mix reaction.

Ten out of thirteen nurses told that Kasturba was good for handling the gynaecological and obstetrics cases besides, for the children health care as well. Rest of the nurses were of the view that they lacked in modern gadgets of treatment if not in the expertise. One of the nurses was quite unhappy with the type of misutilisation of the talent of the nurses taking place in the government hospitals i.e. she had a special training in public health nursing whereas she was not able to utilise her expertise any where in the hospital.

Seven out of seventeen doctors agreed that there is scope for improvement in the indoor wards in terms of behaviour of the staff and in terms of procurement of standard gadgets. The patients and the personnel of hospitals praised for the functioning of Intensive Care Unit and the Cardiac Care Unit of the hospital. The level of efficiency was high in these two units i.e. the patients admitted in these units were terminal ones, secondly they were less in number and above all the best of the man power and gadgets were furnished in these two units. The care and efficiency of treatment did not vary largely in regard to the above mentioned units of M.C.D. hospitals to that of St. Stephens.

So far as the availability of food for indoor cases were concerned, all the patients had full satisfaction in terms of quantity but so far as the quality of food was concerned the patients had one or the other grudge. Mainly the inmates complained of the taste of the food, according to them taste remained mostly unsavoury and according to some the amount of milk they get is not sufficient. Almost every attendant had problem of not getting adequate food so they mainly relied on the food brought from their home.

Health institutions exist but the meaning of these institution does not justify its existence within the over all social system. The people to be served are not being served properly when they visit the hospital. The doctors and other para-medics make the patient follow what they want them to follow without trying to understand the real need of the patient.

The scope, function and meaning of the health care institution will not be understood so long as all the factors, viz, availability, accessibility, affordability and acceptability of the care and cure are not fulfilled. The faith, reliance and anti-prejudicial gesture on both the sides are imperative towards making a sound health culture of the people.

According to the doctors of the Emergency and the Casualty, the doctors said that the complaints have been received in Casualty and

Emergency as well. According to the doctors and nurses of the indoor services, the number of complaints received were as low as ten percent. Most probable reason for less complain was the lack of confidence of the patient to complain or the lack of knowledge regarding the right of an indoor patient.

So far as the dietary do's and don'ts are concerned much care was given for the food and drink of the heart and diabetic patients menu. Although, a dietician was there in each of these government hospital but patients in the general wards were never given adequate food (patients complain) or dietary instruction.

It was not applicable in case of St. Stephens as the food given in that hospital was as per the affordability of the patient, so it was found that the poor patients would not get food brought from their houses but the type of food they are supposed to bring for the patient were determined by the doctor and dietician in advance.

Quite contrary to such practice it was found in the MCD hospitals that as and when the ward aya or ward boy brought milk for patients from kitchen some amount was taken out and kept for their tea club. The same view was endorsed by the patients when they were asked, whether they got adequate milk to drink or not. The reply was in negative. The patients also complained that the nurses were party to such pilferage at times. The patients always wanted some extra food for their attendant and ward boy refused and such refusals always created certain amount of row between the two. The patients said that they requested kitchen staff to bring extra food from the kitchen. Such situation occurred only in M.C.D. hospitals. But, the solution to such problem was some bribe. All round performance of O.P.D. either promotes or tarnishes the image of the hospital. In order to gauge the performance level and efficacy of the O.P.D., exhaustive queries and investigations were conducted at all levels.

Availability of medicine in O.P.D. was of real concern, the patients in O.P.D. were asked about the status of available of medicine at O.P.D, they said unequivocally that for all prescriptions at least one or two medicines were never to be found. Those were to be purchased from the private market. Not a single patient of the O.P.D. was happy with the efficacy of the medicine given in O.P.D. Those who could afford to purchase from market they preferred to have medicine of better quality from the market only. In case of St. Stephens only abjectly poor patients were given medicine from the hospital, whereas the relatively richer patients purchased the medicine from within the hospital pharmacy.

So far as the behaviour of the hospital staff is concerned the doctors of the M.C.D. hospitals fully endorsed that the standard of the O.P.D. has lot of scope for improvement. But according to them much could not be achieved due to lack of streamlining of the local referral system. Doctors and nurses said that there was hardly any scope of improvement in the Emergency and the Casualty. Whereas the doctors agreed that there was scope of improvement in indoor facilities and staff behaviour.

Much talked of ambulatory services for the community was in jeopardy, on asking about the community base services, which they were supposed to render, was being carried out or not. It was found that less than five percent of the health care experts visited Jahangirpuri. School children were asked to bring their younger brothers and sisters below five years of age to the school, where they were vaccinated. The team comprised of one doctor, one nurse one class IV employee. It became conspicuous from the above fact that no one of the staffs were either interested in door to door service or in doing a true community based health care treatment.

Ineffective O.P.D., perfunctory ambulatory services, togather with inadequate referral lead to growth of private practitioner in the colony and the village. In other words, the unmet felt need of the people were unmet due to total mismanaged and callous system of state run hospitals and health services.

Subsequently, this had given rise to a new dimension of institutional health care approach where a myriad of quackery to allopathic health care service were thriving simultaneously even without serving the purpose. The availability of the local institute of health care and accessibility to those were very cumbersome. In other words, those were fulfilling a fraction of their mandate. In one of the previous chapters, it was noted that the people of the colony approached to these places under distress condition or those who could afford to exploit personal relation with the doctors. The general apathy reflected in the behaviour of the doctors and staffs and mechanical approach of treatment with built in prejudice of the doctors and other staffs towards the patients indirectly encouraged the private practitioner to grow rapidly in the area.

Resettlement colonies added a new dimension in private sector health care.

It is worth to mention in this connection the study carried out by Sahu, on tribal community in an industrial set up. He also noted same type of bottlenecks of the state run health care institution. He found, the unskilled, ill-equipped, ill informed, uneducated, ill motivated quacks were having larger vista of operation in Rourkela and its hinterland, at the steel plant though government doctors were equally good in treating the Oraons but their services were never sought after. So far as open market of health care was concerned, it was found by Madan that various reasons can be assigned for the liking and opting out for the private doctors and treatment,

- Effectiveness of treatment
- Cheapness of drug (not always)
- Frequent availability of the doctor
- Customer friendly behaviour.

It was found that eighty percent, irrespective of caste, creed, religion, economic capability rated the efficiency of the medicine dispensed for ailment as unsatisfactory in case of government health service. The factor of cheapness of drug also plays role but on an average five percent opted for cheap drug. Followed by other factors.

In order to know the various loopholes of the system in our institutional health care, a systematic series of observations specially designed questionnaire and purposive conversation were carried out with various echelon of health care staffs.

The responses of the queries are given below :

Forty Eight out of fifty doctors have heard about Jahangirpuri and the village Bhalasawa. According to them, the people of the resettlement were socio-economically poor and lead a life in very unhygienic condition, same number of doctors said that the patients obeyed the instructions given to them only when they were admitted and they tend to forget the same instruction when they were discharged. This kind of behaviour had been attributed to the carelessness of the patient. However, the doctors skill to comunicate was never questioned.

But, when the patients are illiterate or instructions have not been given clearly patients always suffered due to ignorance. Eighteen doctors admitted the fact of communication gap between them and the patient and nearly same amount of the nurses and para-medicos endorsed the fact of communication gap. In case of O.P.D., twenty doctors were ready to admit that patients disenchantment was due to unaccounted loss of time. But in case of emergency both the patient and the doctor were of the view that the services in the emergency were effective. The patient did admit that they did not understand what they were told in O.P.D. or when they were admitted they were in fix. It was admitted by some of the junior doctors that for them to make the patient understand each and every thing was not essential. As they inherited such kind of behaviour from their seniors who by and large did not tell the patient what is his ailment, how much time it will take to get cured, how long one has to stay admitted and why. This behaviour continued resulting in a lot of ground swell amongst the suffering patients and their attendants. This kind of behaviour was not only restricted to the doctors but also deeply rooted in the nurses and in the para-medics as well. Such situation is essentially responsible for creating a good deal of misunderstanding between the patient and the hospital staffs.

It was also noticed very commonly that the senior doctors did find fault with the patient at the first instance rather than with their own juniors. Only one or two doctors during the study in the hospital, admitted that the level of treatment have deteriorated substantially over a period of time. It was told by the doctors of the hospitals that seventy percent of the patients revealed their ailment after a great deal of enquiry and persuation. The same impression could not be had in case of the O.P.D. as both the doctors and the patients admitted that with the given condition of chaos in the O.P.D. it was not possible to give or take better treatment.

It was unanimously reported by the doctors that the patients coming from Jahangirpuri for treatment were poor and some were extremely poor as well. The hygienic condition of these patients were too bad and reasons attributed to such condition was abject poverty of these people. The study showed that those who were extremely poor were not able to utilise the hospitals in the true sense of the term because for them it was available but not accessible or affordable. The prime reason of such paradox was due to restricted contact of such patients with doctor, besides their economic deprivation, these patients were passive recipient of mercy and sympathy of the doctor and staff. On the contrary the economically better off were able to cash their connections and could afford to spend for medicine and other items as when required for getting better deal.

So far as the richer section of the resettlers were concerned, it was said by the doctors that they did not prefer to visit to the MCD run hospitals. Around eighty percent of the cases admitted from the poor section of the people were severe or terminal cases. The above mentioned fact was admitted by all the staffs of the hospital. Such a situation was attributed to two distinct type of thought, the doctors attributed such situation to, (a) The ignorance of the patient regarding their ailment (b) The fear of the alien institution as well as culture where the patient gets lost and feels absolutely helpless. However paradoxical it may seem but such views were only mentioned by the doctors doing house job or young General Duty Medical Officer (G.D.M.O.) but not by the specialists.

This kind of situation compells one to think that such situation is essentially an out come of an alien system which was grafted on this soil to serve a particular section of the society in British India and even today after so many years of independence the situation did not change in spirit but has changed in form. The doctors also admitted the fact that such system of hospital health care leads to more and more complication of treatment as the case does not come in the first instance but he comes after getting dissatisfied from the quacks or the private doctors. And any further mistake to diagnose the case leads to more complication and wastage of time and at times it also proves fatal. So, thirty six out of fifty seven of doctors were of the view that there should be a proper referral at the beginning followed by a systematic and thorough O.P.D. check up. This would not only enhance chances of the patients' survival more but also make the hospital more and more user friendly.

The same number of doctors confirmed the fact that looking into todays cause and effect based treatment and considering the disease as such for the purpose of treatment can not explain the reality of the aliment comprehensively. The social perception of the disease is less meaningful than that of the cause and effect relationship of the disease in the present context of diagnosis. While to improve the patient care service, it is necessary to understand both the clinical and socio-cultural aetiology of the problem or discase.

The doctors were of the view that the chronic cases were Leaving

Against Medical Advise (LAMA) from the hospital, besides a small section of patients who were scared of blood donation or any kind of operation often took the path of LAMA. The cases of LAMA were not so high in case of St. Stephens hospital. The reason being, the care given to the patient in this hospital is of better quality in comparison to that of M.C.D. hospitals. The LAMA cases symbolised the lost faith in the doctor, staff and the institutional health care system. On deep probing it was found that eleven out of fifteen of the doctors felt such a situation is not exclusively the fallacy of the hospital doctors alone. Onus to be shared equally by the local doctors as well. This kind of allegations and counter allegations did not solve the situation, rather it made the whole system more complex at the cost of patients care.

On querying about the patients view regarding the opinion of the performance of nurses and paramedics in the hospital it was found that the patients complained about these staff to the doctors about their negligence and misbehaviour. A section of the patients could not say anything because either they were scared or did not know about their rights (when they go to hospital or get admitted there). The fear psychosis of the patients were very pronounced, more so with the poor patients. The patients did not tell their problems to the well wisher, other than doctor or staff. But the patients after getting convinced, and assured of their safe indoor stay disclosed everything to the scholar but requested not to disclose the conversation because if, such information leaks to the nurse or to the doctor then the patient have to leave the hospital even before getting treated properly (as per the belief of the patient).

Regarding the preferential treatment, forty eight doctors agreed that it was a common practice, some senior doctors said that it was unavoidable because they were bound to help bureaucrats and politicians first, in comparison to those who were poor and helpless. Nurses also endorsed the same view. Quite contrary to the doctors and nurses, the class-IV staff, unanimously said that they helped to those poor and destitute who did not have any one to look after barring few who were ready to serve any time on payment basis only.

Twenty eight out of fifty seven of the doctors said that their performance was not upto the mark in O.P.D. but they had no alternative to such confusion and irregularities.

The management of the missionary hospital was in the hand

of a professional manager, who looked after each and every aspect of the hospital. It was found that the manager was supposed to inculcate the work culture and professionalism in the doctors of the hospital. In contradiction to such attitude the corporation doctors were of the view that the decline of clinical ethics and humanism was mainly due to the cut throat professionalism. Besides, the sense of acute insecurity combined with a lust for more and more earning leading to such carelessness in the treatment of the patient.

The preferential treatment was evident in both types of the hospitals but manifested in different ways. In case of the M.C.D., the doctors were giving extra care to the well known personalities, like political figures, bureaucrats and to their own relatives and acquiantences while in the missionary run it was either religion or status bound. In other words, the poor in both the cases found it difficult to have sympathetic and all round care.

The menace of bribe was common in the municipal corporation run hospitals, according to the doctors they were helpless to stop check such activities. But on the contrary such practices were totally forbidden in St. Stephens hospital.

In St. Stephens Hospital any deviation to the guideline meant invitation to punitive action. This type of measure invariably checks malpractices at the lower level.

The nurses were also interviewed to know the type of feeling they had regarding the patients of Jahangirpuri and about the villagers of Bhalasawa. While trying to know the nurse-patient interaction, it was found that thirty eight out of forty seven of the nurses had heard about the resettlement of Jahangirpuri. Nineteen had seen or visited the colony. Forty two nurses were of the view that their personal hygiene was very bad. Those who visited the colony said that the locality by no means was hygienic to live in. All the nurses were of the opinion that main obstacles of resettlers was the poor economic standard. According to nurses the patients when admitted try to cooperate in their own way so it becomes difficult at time for them (nurses) to interact with the patient. This also reflects that there is a schism between the expected behaviour and actual behaviour as the patients are not primed with such a situation at any stage of their life in most of the cases.

Regarding the loss of time and wage of the poor patient, almost thirty nurses were not happy because according to them it was harassment to patient due to mismanagement of numbering system, ill kept medical records of the cases,. improper referral combined with ignorance of the patient aggravates the situation.

On asking about the overall performance level and the scope to improve the treatment and to enhance the popularity of the hospital, the nurses replied that there is a strong need to change the of behaviour of class IV employees, followed by improvement in the quality and quantity of the gadgets in different wards in order to enchance the image of the hospital. Four nurses were of the view that they should be equiped with newer training and knowledge every three to six month. Such training would help them to give better treatment and care for patients. Only two nurses said that to improve the quality of performance of the hospital there is need of screening at every point and that is possible by charging some amount at the very begining, at O.P.D only.

It was also very important to know from the paramedic and class - IV staff about the performance of the hospital and institutional health care because, majority of these people belonged to poorer section of the society who could project the problem of poor patients very vividly. Moreover, most of the class-IV staff of the hospital have stayed in one of the other resettlement colonies. They were engaged in hospital as sweeper, ward-aya or as ward boy. On asking about the acquaintance with the people of Jahangirpuri, cent percent said that they knew the place and the people. And seventeen out of thirty four of these staff said that they regularly visited the colony on one or the other pretext. According to these people, the hygiene.was not really bad but the people of Jahangirpuri were economically poor. But almost all agreed they could not be ignored as they were also part of the society first and patient there after.

According to class-IV staffs of these hospitals, it was clear that these patients were so scared or shy in nature that they did not talk much when they were admitted. The class IV or the paramedic helped them many a time i.e. they are at times admitted without attendant due to one or the other problem (domestic or financial). The patient need to be taken to latrine or bathroom or sometimes, some medicine to be brought from outside the hospital then no one else could be approached by these patients except for these class-IV staffs.

However, bribes were not taken openly by the class-IV staffs.

But, any help taken by needy patient or attendant or at the time of child birth the concerned patient or mother of the new born or her attendent was pursued to give "Bakshish", a decent way of appropreation of money.

On quality of services given to the patients the paramedics and the class IV rated their respective hospital in high esteem. But according to senior staff the quality of the services have deteriorated than earlier times. The reasons given to such decadency were primarily two, firstly, the increasing pressure of patient and lack of beds at the same time and secondly, the lack of sincerity in the present day doctors to serve patients sincerely. Besides weak Medical Superintendent.

On the question of inter personal behaviour the class-IV and the paramedic told that they always kept amicable relation with the poor and the resettlement colony dwellers. They loose temper with the patients only when they spoil the ward with dirt and filth or in other words when sweepers or any other supportive staff were forced to sweep or clean ward more than twice a day. The study revealed there is large scale mismanagement in the attendance of the regular class-IV employees. The sanitary inspectors of the hospital were getting bribe from the regular class-IV employees and letting them remain missing in duty hours and in those hours of the day these employees were doing extra work and earning extra money from outside hospital. Whereas the adhoc or the daily wage employees were forced to do extra job to compensate the undone work of the regular employees. So, it was obvious that the quality of service given by these people were below standard in most of the cases. This was found to be common complaint in the MCD run hospitals. This type of irregularities were not reported from St. Stephens hospital.

The shortage of drugs seem to be one of the most common phenomena of MCD hospitals. One of the senior ward aya in Hindu Rao told that she of her own had caught personnels of dispensary, who were involved in misappropriation of the medicine from the dispensary and the same was reported by her to the Deputy Medical Superintendent. Although, various threats were given to her by gang of people who were involved in it but she did not keep quiet about the matter. But the Deputy Medical Superintendent did not the take any action against those staffs. And the hospital staff union came to rescue of the the corrupt employees. In these hospitals, it was told that the paramedical staffs do sell out even the cotton bundle, common drugs as well as at times contraceptives were also sold out in bulk to out side shopkeepers.

Regarding the O.P.D. of the hospital, the paramedic and the class IV staff said that the wastage of time by the patients is much more than normal. They also admitted that in cases of acquaintance whoever had approached to them for out of turn consultation or treatment, he or she was helped, more so, when, the patient belonged to their own colony or resettlement. The class-IV and the paramedic opined that the emergency and the casualty services of their hospital were quite prompt and comparable to any good hospital. To maintain indoor more cleaner and tidier they commented that they needed more staffs and as long as the manpower shortage persist, it is difficult to improve the services.

According to many doctors who were enthusiastic to work for the patient found the management of the MCD run hospitals did not give them much liberty to work, moreover, they were also bound by bureaucratic red tapism. On the contrary, the work culture of missionary run hospital was different. It was admitted by few house officers of the missionary hospital that they served more because their service is on contract basis as it was observed by the scholar doctors are not pursuing missionary zeal, even in the missionary hospital inspite of their much publicised motif of "serve the poor and needy".

The study showed the medical social workers were a notional figure for the MCD hospitals rather than being real functionary. The medical social worker in the MCD hospitals were primarily doing the work of an agent of family welfare activities. To help the authorities to detect the real needy patient was not the job of these social workers. The medical social workers along with the O.P.D. doctors were supposed to inpart the health education to the patients. But it was unfortunate to find that the medical social workers in both the hospitals were not carrying out their chartared duties. On the whole, it was realised that even if the patient of Jahangirpuri and the village needed attention when they approached the hospital they were not able to get adequate attention. But unfortunately no one was really ready to admit his or her fault for the fawx pas in patient care.

The lack of space, manpower, gadgets, medicine, laundry items etc. or in other words the problem of logistics and management, besides, the manpower management problem were a chronie feature of these hospitals. Secondly, the socio-cultural barrier between the doctor, nurse and the class-IV or paramedic on one side and the patients on the other (the haitus between the two levels were quite clearly visible when the patient belongs to Jahangirpuri or is from similar type of colonies of the poor socio-economic strata) side of the health care culture spectrum need to be looked into overcome such barrier. Given such type of hospital infrastructure and the institutional health care, besides, the type of privileged class based patient care system, it becomes necessary to go into the overall existing system of institutional health care approach against the back drop of existing socio-cultural milieu of the large chunk of poor patient.

According to Banerji, hospital should be defined in the following manner.... "a hospital is required to become a community institution. This calls for a basic change in the culture of the hospital. It may be emphasised that such a change does not imply that a hospital will cease to offer high technology, services or that there would be any decline in the status of those who provide high technology. A basic change in the culture of a hospital implies essentially a change in the relationship between a technology and community. From inward or westward looking, market dominated, technology oriented institution, the hospital open itself to its requirements by bringing about the necessary reorientation in its technology and in the reorganisation and management." He further added,

> "Hospital thus becomes closely integrated with the entire health services system even while they may be at the apex".... (Banerji 1981). Further more in the same light Banerji said.... "an epidemiological approach to define the role of hospital as a community institution. In other words, activities of hospital becomes an integral part of an overall health strategy involving the use of an "optimised" package of technology promotive, preventive curative and rehabilitative component"....
>
> ....."Having defined the entire range of community health problem, one has to define the health culture of the community, including the felt needs that are generated by various health problems."..... (Banerji).

In the light of above arguments of Banerji, the present study is another effort to understand the reality of resettlement health care set up and institutional care. Moreover, the study is fit for understanding the role of hospitals and dispensaries vis a vis the health culture of Delhi resettlement along with its adjoining areas. This study also gives lot of insight to understand patient within and without hospital, the validity of contemporary hospital as a pedestal of rural-urban health care system. The study also raises the issues to modify the institutional health care in

Indian cities and to make it more meaningful for the needy masses. The role of absolutely passive recipients patient has become a fact of the day. One need to expose the passive role and there after find out an alternative which empowers the system of current health care structure with a vibrant, multifaceted health care model dedicated to patient only. The trauma of hospitalisation for the poor patient is even greater than physical and psychological pains or suffering. The reason for such condition has been explained in the case of the boy with broken leg called Mohan as well as the case of gooddi is equally heartning (vide chapter-5).

The indicator of development in health care remained confound to the bed-patient ratio of hospital, super specialisation, super specialist, advanced technique used for patient care combined with advanced mechanical and technocratic support often governed by bureaucrats who make the institute run as per their needs and desires.

Today the system of institutional health care has become a dehumanised highly technocratised and contractual state apparatus.

There is a lack of understanding on the part of the doctors of patient's; "health culture", in the modern system patient's culture is moulded as per the culture of the institution and when the patient do not confirm to such effort of the doctor, he is blamed, neglected and ignored. This has resulted in loss of credeniality and accountability in the present health care system.

All these together have led to a status of confusion and confrontation within and without the system of health care.

As Antia[5] puts.... "We are informed that the large urban public hospitals are for the care of the poor and needy who cannot afford private medical care and that the affiliated medical colleges are there to produce the doctors who will look after the health of our people. The plethora of reports about the rank inefficiency, callousness and inhuman conditions that prevail in these institutions....demostrates that the poor are only there to justify the construction and running of such hospitals. The only time any attempt is made to provide effective service is when a politician, bureaucrat, doctor, or their relations and friends, require free service, for, these hospitals have become free private nursing homes for the rich and influentials...." He further adds,

....."The facilities and training provided is therefore in keeping with the

> requirement of private practice among the affluent section of our society and their pattern of diseases, rather than with the requirement of the vast majority which lives in rural India or even in the urban slums".

Antia has also raised the issue of medical teaching and training of the doctors in hospitals..... "There is not a single general practitioner in the large hospital who can teach the student, the care of common illness and demonstrate how to sort out the few cases requiring more specialised care. This duty is left to the sweet will of the clerk who issues the O.P.D. papers. Even the staff of such institution finds difficulty in locating the myriad department and one can imagine the plight of the poor without any of advise or guide in the medical maze".....

In this connection he also mentioned that,.... "The large urban hospital with its affiliated medical colleges are therefore institutions designed more for the benefit of medical profession the politician and the medical industry rather than for the poor. Besides, large institutions by their very nature are impersonal and not keeping with our very personalised culture"......

While suggesting an alternative to such a system of health care, he said.

> ......"What the vast majority of our people require are small thirty to sixty bed hospitals situated within easy reach of the community and where the majority of the basic as well as referral problems of local population can be attended to, in a human atmosphere, leaving only a very few difficult problems for the urban apex hospital".... (Anita)

Of late various committees recommended plethora of small and big reports, decisions have been taken to build hundred bedded hospitals in various resettlement colonies. Since, the inception of .he colony of Jahangirpuri it was also decided by the authorities that the colony should be provied with such a hospital, for the benefit of colony as well as for the adjoining village. Inspite of building of hospital in the early nineties the health care status of the resettlere and the villagers did not improve substantially (inspite of door step care) as the health care structure of the institutes were not made people oriented and it lacks a long overdue humane outlook of care givers and the system administrators, it could not attract the people of its own rather the patients visited under exigency and in utter confusion.

Such a situation reflects a lack of political will to make the community hospitals which can serve the need of the community, health culture conscious, institutional health care system is still a dream to materialise for the needy mass.

As, Banerji, has said that the health status of the people is always maintaining a kind of dynamic equilibrium and to keep the equilibrium in proper order there is a need of purposive intervention by the state, and these are only possible when the steps taken are well timed and well accepted as well. Todays, lackadaisical hospital health care system of Delhi and other big cities are outcome of an alien system grafted into a non western health system with no major concern of its being adopted or accepted by the masses. The situation is getting more and more exacerbated by building a superstructure of highly dehumanised, technocratic professional, parochial and commercial cadre of specialists who is turn looks after the interest of few.

The present study has found ample situation of confusion and so it warrants a serious thinking on the part of our policy planners and administrators for making the dispensaries and hospital an integral part of people's health culture which in turn would be an inseperable and acceptable part of the resettlers and rural people's health culture and the community.

7

SUMMARY

The aim of the study was to investigate the role of hospitals and local dispensaries in determining the health culture of Delhi's resettlement colony, as well as peripheral village of the metropolis. The adjoining village was considered for the study to find out the impact of the village's economy or health culture influence on the resettlement colony. Moreover, an idea could be had by the study, did change occur in terms of health care in the village due to the establishment of institutional health care organs (state and private run) in the resettlement colony. Such a study not only speaks of a particular case or scenario but it also helps understand the overall status of the health care position in the metropolitan resettlement in particular and peripheral village in general.

The resettlement has both types of health care facilities public as well as private one. The state run dispensaries are mainly managed and controlled by Delhi Administration and Municipal Corporation of Delhi. Delhi Administration dispensaries are the general care institutions and the corporation run are primarily meant for mother and Child Health Care, as well as for family planning activities. There is also provision of an Ayurvedic dispensary run by Municipal Corporation within the colony other than already mentioned health care facilities. Besides, there is one dispensary run by Employees State Insurance Scheme to serve the health care needs of the factory or mill workers and their families.

The private clinics being run by both qualified and semiqualified doctors of various type i.e., Allopathic, Homeopathic, Ayurvedic etc. the people of the colony and the village visit them and those health care institutions also made a part of the present study.

The colony has eleven blocks, which are endowed with schools, markets, bus stops, banks, police station and industrial training institute, whereas, the village has none of these facilities within its premises rather it depends on the resettlement for the above mentioned facilities.

The inhabitants of Jahangirpuri comprised of wide sprectum of people who have come from various parts of Delhi i.e. north and east Delhi and from outside Delhi as well. These people hailed from all walks of life, caste religious groups and economic sections. They were engaged in various activities, viz, vending vegetable and fruits, selling knick knacks and toys in various colonies, working as wheeler dealer, working as porter at various places from warehourse to road construction, as household servants (mostly the women) and seller of variety of items on commission basis right on the pavement in various market places and also engaged in other odd an sundry activities. And a small section of people work as government servants, as well as working a handful few are in private sectors.

More than eighty percent of the population of the colony comprised of the Hindu followed by the Muslim and the Sikh respectively. More than sixty percent of the households were Hindi speaking, thirty five percent of the inhabitants were Punjabi speaking and two percent of the colony dwellers were Bengali speaking. It showed that such resettlements are highly heterogenious in nature.

The people of the colony were originally migrants from Uttar Pradesh, Haryana, Rajasthan, Madhya Pradesh and West Bengal and a very small fraction from Tamil Nadu also came and settled here.

Majority were living in 23 square yard plots. Only the rich were living in 46 square yard. On average seventy percent of the people were staying in one room apartment.

Community latrines were used by the people as independent domestic latrines were not provided due to lack of proper sewage system. However, of late the w/c latrine been provided in most of the houses. The colony did not have neat and clean park or lawn for children, so they were playing on the lanes. The colony was full of open gutters, as a result both the colony and the village was full of mosquitoes and flies. And a large number of stray cattles and street dogs could be seen in both the resettlement and the village.

Although the people of the colony were practising their own cultural at home but out of their own four wall it was the pot-purri of resettlement culture. However, a certain degree of commonality of cultural intermix of traits can be observed in various sphere of life amongst the resettlers.

An effort has been made to understand the meaning, perception and behaviour of the health and health care practices of the people with the given background of their society and culture. The study of the health culture has been understood by making an in-depth study of the meaning attributed to the disease by the people and the behaviours of the people towards understanding and ameliorating the ailment and the various practices adopted by the people in their own way to get relief from any disease.

In order to understand the health and culture of the people, a comprehensive assessment was done by determining the mechanism of the state intervention and the role of state apparatus in shaping the health culture and behaviour of the people.

The main findings were on the health culture parameters of the people of Jahangirpuri and Bhalasawa in the light of, the role being played by existing health care institutions (however restricted may it be) to sustain and support healthy living of these people. Hospitals response to various health problems, besides, people's active effort to get redressal outside their own culturally determined health care practices, were also part of the present study.

It was found that very large proportion of their felt need in case of health care services remained unmet because of limitations in their access (not merely physical) to these health care institutions combined with limited affordability (in terms of purchasing power). Eventhough, the institutes such as local government dispensaries and hospital were available but were yet to be accepted in true sense of the term, as because for these resettlers and peripheral villagers of the metropolis, they are disadvantaged by urban laws or code of conduct of day to day life affairs, which prevents them to practice their own, lifestyle and familiar activities. Their lives are made difficult, because of conflicts with the codes of urban law reinforced by the strappings of elitist code of conduct. Many public institutions and services are just not in reality available to these people. In practice, these are out of the reach of the people for whom it is primarily meant. The poor only use these for livelihood (though not always), not to avail the services of those institutions. This is because these are designed by and for urban elitist minded people; or there is just not enough as services are expensive to be afforded. In short to serve, the purpose of these people the system needs to be purposively redesigned, in such a fashion which provides the system no means to mystify the basics of health care and thereby serve the cause aptly and meaningfull.

Control of the health institutions were from the top which determined the health care behaviour of the people. Moreover, the institutes which were in existence within and without the colony were strictly governed by the dictums of trickle down in terms of policy, planning and practice of health care, their very existence was not effective for the local health care seekers. Such uncertainity was evident from the fact that even those who had provision of free health care facility in the local dispensaries, i.e. MCD dispensary, E.S.I. or in the hospital were not better off in terms of health care status than those, who did not posses any such health care facility.

Ineffective system and treatment process have generated sufficient amount of apathy towards the facade of available free health care. Moreover, the desire to fulfil unmet felt need of the population in relation to their day to day health problem have created a market for private practitioners of allopathic system as well as for the quackery.

Due to such lukewarm attitude of the system the resettlers were compelled to make strenuous effort at times to get minimum basic health care facilities. On the contrary such effort was daubed by the personnals of the system as the fault of the people. In other words, victim blaming is an easy solution for the failure of state apparatus.

The study showed that there is a hiatus between the two levels of the sub-culture complex namely, "health culture" of the people and the "institutional sub-culture". The reason of such gap is built into the system of our modern day institutional health care. So, it demands an intervention of more pragmatic nature to make the whole system much more user friendly and answerable to the very society of which it is a part and parcel.

REFERENCES

Antia N.H., *Indian Express*, 6 June.

Banerji D., *Hospital and promotion in Community Participation in Primary Health Care CIDA*, Karachi 1981.

Madan T.N., "Who choses modern modern medicine and why" *The Social and Cultural Context of Medicine in India*, Vikas Publishing, 1981.

Sahu S.K., *Health Culture of Organs of Rourkela and Hinterland*: C.S. M.C.H., J.N.U., 1980, New Delhi.

Valentine. C, *Culture and Poverty Critique and Counter Proposals*, Chicago. The university of Chicago Press.

BIBLIOGRAPHY

Advani, M. (1980), *Doctor Patient Relationship in Indian Hospitals*; Sanghi Advani Jaipur, 1980.

Antia N.H., *Big Hospitals for Whose Benefit*. Indian Express (Delhi Ed.) 6th June, 1988.

---------- (1989), *Hospital or Health*, Bombay, FRCH.

Banerji, D. (1971), *Family Planning in India: A Critique and Perspective*, Peoples Publishing House, New Delhi.

----------(1981), *Hospital and Promotion in Cummunity Participation in Primary Health Centre CIAD* (Karachi Meet) Pakistan, Karachi.

---------- (1982), *Poverty. Class and Health Culture*, Prachi Publication, New Delhi.

---------- (1986), *Health and Family Planning Services in India: An Epidemiological. Socio-Cultural and Political Analysis & Perspective*, Lok Paksh, New Delhi.

---------- (1986), *Social Sciences and Health Service Development in India: Sociology of Formation of an Alternative Paradigm*, Lok Paksh, New Delhi.

---------- (1990), *A Socio-cultural. Political and Administrative Analysis of Health Policies and Programmes in India in Eighties: A critical appraisal.* Lok Paksh, New Delhi.

Bhore, Joseph et.al., *National Health Survey and Development Committee Ministry of Health*, G.O.I, New Delhi (Vol. I-IV)

Borkar, G. (1957), *Health in Independent India*. Ministry of Health. G.O.I., New Delhi.

Caudiil, W. (1953), *Applied Anthropology Today Ed. A.L. Kroeber*. University of Chicago Press, Chicago.

Chattopadhya, D. (1977), *Science and Society in Ancient India*, Research India Publication, Calcutta.

Chatterjee, Meera (1988), *Implementing Health Policy.* New Delhi, Manohar Publications.

Chaudhury, Z. (1982), *An Experiment in Basic Service Delivery in Devloping Countries.* A view from Ganosetya Kendra, Bangladesh, HOW NOO, 1982; 11-18.

Coe, R.M. (1970), *Medical Sociology;* McGraw-Hill Book Company.

Deasi, A.R.& Pillai, S.D. (ed), *A Profile of an Indian Slum;* Asia Publishing House, Bombay.

Desai, P.B. (1985), *An Overview of Health Policy,* Delhi Institute of Economic Growth.

Delhi Administration (1985), *Delhi Statistical Hand-Book;* Delhi Bureau of Economics and Statistics.

Djurfeldt, G. and Lindberg, S. (1975), *Pills against Poverty: A Study of the Introduction of Western Medicine in Tamil Village;* Curzon Press, Lund Sweden.

Engles Friedrich and Marx Karl (1978), *Communist Manifesto*, Progress Publisher, Moscow.

Freeman, H.E. and Levin, S. (1972), *A Handbook of Medical Sociology.* Prentice Hall, New Jersy.

Freidson, E. (1971), *Profession of Medicine: A Study of the Sociology of Applied Knowledge;* Herper & Row, New York.

Foster, G.M. and Anderson, B.G., *Medical Anthropology*, John Wiley and Sons, New York.

Freire, P. (1972), *Pedagogy of the Oppressed,* Penguin Book Co., London.

Ganguly, K.K. (1985), *A Sociological Study: Hospital in India*; J.N.U. News Letter, New Delhi.

----------(1989), "Indian Hospitals in the Context of Health for all- A.D. 2000"; *Health and Family Welfare Service in India.*. Asia Publishing House, New Delhi; B. Jena & R.N. Pati (Ed.).

---------- (1990), "Indian Hospital: A Cultural Interphase": *Medical Anthropology.* Joshi P.C. & Mahajan A (Ed). Reliance Publishing House, New Delhi.

Gish,Oscar (1976), *Medical Brain Drain Revisited;* International Journal of Health Services.

George, Susan (1977), *How the Other Half Dies.* Pelican Books, Harmondsworth, U.K.

Gladstone Iago (1965), *Medicine in Transition:* Chicago University Press, Chicago.

Gopalan, C. (1983a), *A Nutrition Policy of Brinkmanship,* Nutrition Foundation of India Bulletin, New Delhi.

Goodee, W.J. and Hatt, P.K. (1952), *Methods in Social Research,* McGraw Hill Book Co., Tokyo.

Gould, H.A. (1957), *The Implication of Technological Change for Folk and Scientific Medicines:* American Anthropologist: 59: 507-518.

Green Stephen (1974), *The Hospital; An Organisational Analysis:* Blackie; London.

Gupta, G.R. (Ed.) (1981), *The Main Events of Indian Sociology Vol.-IV: The Social and Cultural Context of Medicine in India:* Vikas Publishing House, New Delhi.

Hassan, K.A. (1979), *Medical Sociology of Rural India.* Sachin Publication; Ajmer.

Illich Ivan (1976), *Limits of Medical Newisis: The Expropritation of Health.* Fenguine Books, Harmondsworth, U.K.

Indina Council Medical Research (1980), *Evaluation of Primary Health Programmes,* Proceedings of the National Conference Held in April 1980, ICMR, New Delhi.

ICMR, ICSSR (1979), *Alternative Approaches to Health Care,* New Delhi, ICMR.

ICSSR and ICMR (1981), *Health for all: Am Althernative Strategy,* Pune, Indian Instititute of Education.

Jeffery, Roger (1979), *"Recognising India's Doctors. The Establishment of Medical Dependency 1918-1939",* Modern Asian Studies B, 301-326.

---------- (1980), *Medical Policy Making in India in the 1970. Out of Dependency?* Colloques Internationaux du C.N.R.S. No. 582, 525-530.

---------- (1988), *Politics of Health in India,* Berkeley: University of California Press, California.

Kirkpatrick, J. (1981), "The Delivery of Hospital Services in North India, Punjab, Ludhiana: A Client Institution Interaction Model, 125-49", *Main Currents in Indian Sociology,* Vol. IV, Vikas Publishing

House, New Delhi.

Landy David (Ed) (1977), *Culture, Disease and Healing.* Macmillan Publishing Co., New York.

Lal, S.K. and Chandini, A. (1987), *Medical Care: Readings in Medical Sociology.* Jainsons Publication, New Delhi.

Leninger, M. (1970), *Nursing and Anthropology, Two world to Blend:* Johan Wiley and Sons, Inc. New York.

Leslie Charse (ed) (1976), *Asian Medial System: A Comparative Study:* University of California Press, California.

Lewis Oscar (1966), *La Vida, A Puertarican Family in Culture of Poverty.* San Juan and New York; New York, Random House.

Loudon, J.B. (Ed) (1976), *Social Anthropology and Medicine,* Academic Press, London.

Madan, T.N. (Ed) (1980), *Doctors and Society.* Vikas Publishing House, New Delhi.

Marriot Mackim (Ed) (1953), *Village India.* Chicago University Press, Chicago.

Mathur, Indu (1975), *Human Organisation of a Hospital.* Alkh Publications, Jaipur.

Mathews C.M.E. (1979a), *Health and Culture in South Indian Village.* Sterling Publisher, New Delhi.

Malachan, G. and Makcown, T. (Ed) (1972), *Medical History and Medical Care.* Oxford University Press, London.

Machanich David (1978), *Medical Sociology.* Free Press, New York.

Ministry of Health and Family Welfare (1982-83), *Annual Report.* Govt. of India Press, New Delhi.

Mudaliar, A. (1962), *National Health Survey and Planning Committee Ministry of Health.* Govt. of India. (Vol. I & II), New Delhi.

Mumford, E. (Jr.) and Skipper, K. (Jr.) (1967), *Sociology in Hospital Care,* Harper and Row, New York.

Munshi, S. (Ed) (1989), *Urbanization Growth of Slum Social Conflict and Environment Hazard.*

----------, *Report of National Seminar;* Joshi Adhikari Institute of Social Studies, New Delhi.

Myrdal, G. (1968), *Asian Drama: An Enquiry into the Poverty of Nations*. New York, Penguin Books.

National Institute of Health and Family Welfare, Health Sector in India, An Overview; NIHFW, New Delhi.

Navaro, V. (Ed) (1976), *Allendes Chil: A Case Study in the Breaking of Underdevelopment Medicine Under Capitalism*, Nealse Watson, New York.

Nichter, M. (1980), *Health Expenditure Report*. New Delhi, USAID.

Nurullah, S. and Naik, J.D. (1957) and Co. Ltd., *A History of Education in India During British Period*, Macmillan.

Oommen, T.K. (1978), *Doctors and Nurses*, Macmillan Publishing House, New Delhi.

Park, J.E. and Park, K. (1980), *Text Book Preventive and Social Medicine;* M.S. Banarasi Das Jabalpur.

Parson, T. (1949), *The Structure of Social Action*. Amerind Publishing Co. Pvt. Ltd., New Delhi.

Pathak, S. (1979), *Social Welfare Health and Family Planning in India.*

Paul, B.D. (Ed) (1955), *Health, Culture and Community Case Studies Public Reaction to Health Programmes*. Russel Sage Foundation, New York.

Poyenter, N. (1971), *Medicine and Man*. Penguin Books, Middlesex, U.K.

Qadeer, I. (1985), Social Dynamics of Health Care: The Community Health Worker Scheme in Shadol District, *Socialist Health Review*, Vol.-II, No.2.

Ramalingaswami, P. (1972), *Studies on Medical Students*, NIHAE, New Delhi.

Rivers, W.H. (1924), *Medicine Magic and Religion*, Kegan Paul & Co. Ltd., London.

Rosengren, W. (1980), *Sociology of Medicine. Harper and Medical Care.* Russel Sage Foundation, New York.

Saunders, R. (1954), *Cultural Differences and Medical Care*, Russel Sage Foundation, New York.

Schwartz, H.D. and Kart, C.S. (Ed), *Dominant Issues on Medical Anthropology*, Addison Wesley Publication Co., New York.

Seal, S.C. (1975), *Health Administration in India:* Dawn Books, Calcutta.

Sen, Amaritya and Sengupta, Sunil, "Malnutrition of Rural Children and Sex Bias". *Economic and Political Weekly*. Annual Report, Bombay.

Sukhatme, P.V. (1980), "Nutrition Policy: Need for Reorientation". *Economic and Political Weekly*, / Vol. XV, No. 26, June, 29.

Tandon, B.N. (1980), *Integrated Child Development Services in India.* A.I.I.M.S., New Delhi.

Tappan, F.M. (1968), *Towards Understanding Administration in the Medical Environment*, Macmillan Co., New York.

Taylor, C. (Ed) (1976), *Doctors for the Village. Study of Rural Intership in Several Indian Medical Colleges*, Asia Publishing House, Bombay.

Timmapaya, A. (1972), *Serarch in District Health Administration.* Rohtak, NIHAE, New Delhi.

Trakroo, P.L. et al. (1977), *"Reaction of Patients Towards the Evening OPD Services in Hospitals of Delhi.* NIHAE, Bulletin, Vol. 10, No. 4, pp. 293-302.

Tuckett David (Ed) (1976), *An Introduction to Medical Sociology:* Tavistock Publication; London.

Valentine, C. (1972), *Culture and Poverty Critique and Counter-Proposals. Chicago,* The University of Chicago Press.

Venkataratnam, R. (1979), *Medical Sociology Indian Setting*, Macmillian, Madras.

Voluntary Health Association of India (1987), *Elements of National Health Policy.* VHAI, New Delhi.

Van der-Veen, K.W., Van der Sjakk Geest (Ed) 1979), *In Search of Health. Essays in Medical Anthropology.* University of Amsterdam.

Whyte William, F. (1943), *Street Corner Society,* University of Chicago Press, Chicago.

World Health Organisation, (1975), *Health by the People*, W.H.O. Publication, Geneva.

---------- (1975), *Technical Reports Series on "Hospital" Geneva.* W.H.O.

---------- (1985), *Issues Concerning Hospital at the First Referral Level: Expert Committee on the Role of Hospital at the First Level.*

Geneva. 17th Dec. (SHS/EC/85.3) pp. 1-10.

Wright Mills, C. (1980), *The Sociological Imagination:* Penguin Books Ltd., Harmondsworth, U.K.

Weber Max (1946), *Essays in Sociology*. Oxford, University Press, Oxford.

Zurbrigg Sheila (1984), *Rekku's Story: Structures of Ill Health and the Source of Change Bangalore*. Centre for Social Action.

THESES AND JOURNALS

Anand, R.C. (1974), *A Comparative Study of Emergency Services in Three Large Delhi Hospitals*. National Institute of Health Administration and Education, New Dehli.

Anand, D. & Rama Rao, A. (1963), *How Well Doctors Communicate - A Diagnostic Study:* Indian Journal of Public Health 7(3), pp. 152-156.

Advani, M. and Aggarwal, K.G. (1973), *Dimension of Hospital in Social System: Hospital and Its People*. NIHAE:

Avasthi, A., *The Public Hospital Cases and Indian Administrators:* Indian Institute of Public Administration.

Banerjee, J.N. (1966), History of Medical Teaching in India from the Pre-literary Period upto Modern Times, *Indian Journal of Medical Education* 5: pp. 79-90.

Bhatia, A.K., (1970), Needs and Problems of Patients, *The Nursing Journal of India*. New Delhi.

Bordia, A.K. (1967), Doctor Patient Relationship. *Journal of India*. Medical Association 48(5), 210-212.

Jain, A.P. et al. (1968), *Report of the Study Groups on Hospitals. Ministry of Health and Family Planning and Urban Development*. New Delhi.

Khosla, J.N. et al. (1969), *Citizen and Hospital Administration*. Indian Institute of Public Administration. New Delhi.

Kuppuswami, T.N. (1978), *Patients and Hospitals*, NIHAE, Vol. VIII, No. 1.

Majumdar, Krishna (1978), *Socio-Psycho Economic Problems Among Hospital Patients of West Bengal*, Culcutta University, Calcutta.

Megaw, J.W.D. and Bhutt, E. (Ed), "Medicine and Public Health in India",

Social Service in India. London. His Majesties Stationery Office, pp. 181-215.

Minocha, Aneeta (1974), *Some Aspects of the Social System of an Indian Hospital*. Delhi University, Delhi.

Nathan, R. (1904), *Progress of Education in India*. 1897-98, 1901-1902, Vol. (2).

Prabhatamma, C. & Sharma, S., *Medical Sociology. Some Problems of Study*. The Economic and Political Weekly, Bombay, 17: 1797-98.

Sahu, S.K. (1980), *Health Culture Oraons of Rourkela and Hinterland: Centre for Social Medicine and Community Health*. J.N.U., New Delhi.

Shau, S.K. (1985), *"Socio-Cultural Dimensions of Health Disease and Family Welfare in India"*. Bharatiya Samajik Chintan, Vol.-VIII No. 34.

Rao, K.N. et al. (1968), *Report of the Hospital Review Committee (Delhi Hospitals)*. Ministry of Health and F.P. and Urban Development, New Delhi.

Richey, J.A. (1922), *Selection for Education Records*. 1840-59, (Part-II). Super Govt. Printing, Calcutta.

Sarbadhikari, K.C. (1962), *Western Medical Education in India during the Early Days of British Occupation*. Indian Journal of Medical Education 1:27-32.

Shah, A.M. (1967), *Doctor Patient Relationship. Journal of Indian Medical Association*. New Delhi 49 (4), 194-96.

Satayanaryana Rao, A.V. (1979), *The Organisation and Management of Teaching Hospitals in Andhra Pradesh: Case Study of Osmania General Hospital*. Dept. of Public Administration. University of Hyderabad.

Sharma, Prema (1974), *Cultural Factors of Childhood Diseases: A Study in Medical Sociology*. Lucknow University, Lucknow.

Trakroo, P.L. (1980), *Social Pattern of Seeking Medical Care: A Study of Cultural Behvaiour in Rural India*, New Delhi.

Thomas, A. (1966), *Patient Centred Nursing Case:* College of Nursing (Memiograph), New Delhi.

GOVERNMENT OF INDIA REPORTS

All India Institute of Medical Sciences, *National Workshop on Hospital Planning and Design*. 4-6 Feb., New Delhi, AIIMS.

Government of India (1980), *Sixth Five Year Plan G.O.I.*, 1980-85, New Delhi Planning Commission.

---------- (1985a), *Seventh Five Year Plan G.O.I.*, 1986-90, New Delhi Planning Commission.

Government of India (1973), *Report of the Committee on M.P.W.*, New Delhi, Ministry of Health and Family Planning.

---------- (1982a), *Statements on National Health Policy*. New Delhi, Ministry of Health and Family Welfare.

---------- (1975), *"Group on Medical Education and Support Manpower Health Services and Medical Education: A Programme for Immediate Action. Report*. New Delhi, Ministry of Health and Family Planning.

Indian Council of Medical Research (1980), *Evaluation of Primary Health Programme*. Proceedings of National Conference Held in April, 1980, ICMR.

N.I.H.F.W. (1985), *Study of Referral Services*. N.I.H.F.W., New Delhi.

National Planning Committee (1949), *Sub-Committee on National Health*, Report, Bombay, Vora.

Rural Health Research Centre. (1972). R.H.R.C., Narangwal, Report.

INDEX

❑❑❑